CIRCLE SOLUTIONS FOR STUDENT WELLBEING

Education at SAGE

SAGE is a leading international publisher of journals, books, and electronic media for academic, educational, and professional markets.

Our education publishing includes:

- accessible and comprehensive texts for aspiring education professionals and practitioners looking to further their careers through continuing professional development

- inspirational advice and guidance for the classroom

- authoritative state of the art reference from the leading authors in the field

Find out more at: **www.sagepub.co.uk/education**

CIRCLE SOLUTIONS FOR STUDENT WELLBEING

2nd Edition

Sue Roffey

Los Angeles | London | New Delhi
Singapore | Washington DC

Los Angeles | London | New Delhi
Singapore | Washington DC

SAGE Publications Ltd
1 Oliver's Yard
55 City Road
London EC1Y 1SP

SAGE Publications Inc.
2455 Teller Road
Thousand Oaks, California 91320
SAGE Publications India Pvt Ltd

B 1/I 1 Mohan Cooperative Industrial Area
Mathura Road
New Delhi 110 044

SAGE Publications Asia-Pacific Pte Ltd
3 Church Street
#10-04 Samsung Hub
Singapore 049483

Editor: Jude Bowen
Editorial assistant: Rachael Plant
Production editor: Nicola Marshall
Copyeditor: Elaine Leek
Proofreader: Emily Ayers
Indexer: David Roffey
Marketing manager: Lorna Patkai
Cover design: Naomi Robinson
Typeset by: C&M Digitals (P) Ltd, Chennai, India
Printed and bound in Great Britain by
Ashford Colour Press Ltd, Gosport, Hampshire

Starter list of strengths   p. 32
What happened?   p. 63
Perspectives   p. 65
Punch lines   p. 70
Lists A and B   p. 72
What do we know?   p. 76
Coded sentence   p. 77
Cat rescue   p. 80
Our rights and responsibilities   p. 91
Fair or unfair?   p. 93
Child crying   p. 97

Library of Congress Control Number: 2013940978

British Library Cataloguing in Publication data

A catalogue record for this book is available from
the British Library

ISBN 978-1-4462-7284-8
ISBN 978-1-4462-7285-5 (pbk)

Contents

List of Photocopiable Resources

About the Author

Previously a teacher and educational psychologist, Sue Roffey is currently Adjunct Associate Professor at the University of Western Sydney and Honorary Lecturer at University College London and now lives between Sydney and London. She is a prolific author, international educational consultant and speaker on issues related to pro-social behaviour, belonging, resilience and positive relationships within education. She is the founder and director of Wellbeing Australia (www.wellbeingaustralia.com.au/wba). Sue can be contacted at: www.sueroffey.com/sue and www.circlesolutions network.com/csn.

Preface

This book was first published as *Circle Time for Emotional Literacy* in 2006.

There has been a wealth of new evidence on wellbeing in the last decade and this new edition reflects our developing knowledge about factors that help us flourish, be resilient, form healthy relationships and be active, engaged learners.

Circle Time has moved on and Chapter 1 explains the change of name to Circle Solutions (CS). This edition has more detailed guidance on the quality of facilitation and encouragement to apply both the principles of the Circle philosophy and the learning from Circle sessions in everyday classroom practice. We need to teach social and emotional learning (SEL) in a context that is aligned and not counterproductive. If we want students to have positive relationships this needs to be modelled in the way we all relate to each other, together with congruent school priorities and policies. The framework in Appendix 1 provides twelve dimensions for the content of SEL together with suggestions for a context that will maximize sustainable outcomes. The evidence suggests that if you are embracing Circle Solutions fully you will be growing great kids and growing great schools.

This new edition has additional themes in some of the chapters and more emphasis on strengths and solutions. There is a totally new chapter on positive thinking, using fictional characters to personify positive and negative thoughts.

Readers who have a copy of the original will notice that although some activities are the same or have been adapted, several have been omitted to make space for new ones. Teachers starting out with Circles will still find everything they need to ensure that Circles go well in their class but experienced practitioners will also find activities to expand their repertoire of ideas.

You are encouraged to use this book creatively. Develop the ideas here and try out new things – make a note of those that work and perhaps put them up on the Circle Solutions website, www.circlesolutionsnetwork.com/csn, so everyone can benefit. Repetition of activities can be useful to both familiarize students and also reinforce learning.

Note that the words teacher, facilitator and leader are used interchangeably as are student and pupil. Both apply to children and young people from pre-school to Year 12. CS is a philosophy and pedagogy not a program – the content is your choice to meet the age and needs of your class or group.

The letters Y, M and S indicate whether an activity is most suitable for younger children (Y), middle childhood (M) or seniors (S) (students in high school). Each **YMS** activity has been labeled (as in margin) to show you what age group it is most appropriate for. The framework can also apply to staff meetings, student councils and anywhere else where there is group interaction.

Please invite others into your Circle from time to time (parents, grandparents, school governors) so they know what Circles are about and why you are doing this. Encourage students to work together to plan and run Circles in other classes – especially some of our 'double whammy' kids, those who experience adversity in their lives and who are likely to be more challenging as a result. Ensure they have enough support to do this well. It is a real confidence booster.

If you facilitate Circles according to the principles of CS – give students agency, show them respect, focus on solutions and have fun – not only will your pupils begin to learn how to be and how to live well with others, you are likely to find that your relationship with them also changes, giving your own wellbeing a much deserved boost!

Acknowledgements

My thanks go to those many educators who have shared their ideas with me and taken Circle Solutions to heart in their schools. Participants on Trainer courses from all over the world have been particularly motivating and I have learnt from you all. Forgive me for not crediting everyone by name, but Kirsti Elliott deserves a special mention for compiling the original Index of Games developed further in this edition, and Sam Kourakis for inspiring the Circles Solutions film for parents in her school.

My associates Ali Palmer and Bill Hansberry are dear friends and colleagues, dedicated to student wellbeing. They have been running CS courses in South Australia and Queensland very successfully for several years now. Ali and Bill have read and helpfully critiqued every chapter of this new edition and Ali has also been a stalwart personal support. She is a dynamo of creativity and compassion, living what she teaches. I also want to thank Kerry Bird, not only for what she does for relationship building in Catholic Education but for becoming my touchstone for how to be in the world.

Wellbeing Australia is a network of organizations and individuals determined to keep social and emotional wellbeing as a core value in education. It is a pleasure to work with those who personify the values of collaboration, positive communication and friendship. We have now joined with the Australian Research Alliance for Children and Young People (ARACY) to form SWAN – the Student Wellbeing Action Network.

Madelene McGrath, Kathryn Bermingham, Pat Doolan and many others in Dubbo have been champions of the Aboriginal Girls Circle – an initiative auspiced by the National Association for the Prevention of Child Abuse and Neglect. They have been resolute in getting it going, keeping it going and developing the philosophy of Circle Solutions throughout the Dubbo community. I have had such a great time working with you all. Hopefully what we have managed to achieve will develop further afield in coming years. My appreciation to Dr Brenda Dobia and her team at the University of Western Sydney and Professor Florence McCarthy for their work on evaluation.

As always, my thanks go to Jude Bowen at SAGE, who not only has great professional competence but has also been a constant supporter of my work for nearly fifteen years.

My husband, David, allows me to concentrate on the creative process and meeting deadlines while he does the donkey work of formatting, proof-reading, checking references and making dinner. I hope I tell him often enough how much I love and value him!

And finally, to the children and young people themselves. The future lies with you. So many of you have taken the learning from Circles to develop new ways of being in the world, to be more supportive of each other, to become confident enough to be leaders, to make decisions that are not just about self interest but what we can do together to build healthier schools and stronger communities for everyone. You are my inspiration; you are our hope, this is for you.

1

The Circle Solutions Philosophy and Principles

This introductory chapter provides an overview of the history and theoretical foundations for Circle interventions and a summary of research on authentic wellbeing. Circle Solutions are embedded in a philosophy that impacts not only on activities, but also on their implementation and the context in which they take place.

Circles in History

The symbolism of circles is ageless. A circle can represent wholeness, continuity, universality, unity, inclusion, equality and protection. Using a circle formation as a means of social interaction is both historical and cross-cultural. The North American medicine wheel is just one example of how traditionally indigenous communities have used circles as a means of decision-making and conflict resolution. The 'Quality Circle' initiative, first developed by Kaoru Ishikawa in Japan in the 1960s (Ishikawa, 1980), has been used widely in a business environment. It is based on the principle that full participation in decision-making and problem-solving improves the quality of work. Circles are now also an essential feature of the restorative justice movement, involving all who have been affected by an offence, including the offender.

Development of Circles in Education

I first came across Circles in 1991 in a school in New Jersey. The principal told me that each class held a 'Magic Circle' every day and how this made a positive difference across the school. Others have since taken up and developed the Circle framework. It is known by many names, including Circle Time, Tribes, Learning Circles and now Circle Solutions. Much of this book builds on the ideas of Jenny Mosley, Marilyn Tew, Murray White, Bob Bellhouse, Tina Rae and others. Like language, the Circle framework is constantly evolving, with contributions from many educators.

Why 'Circle Solutions'?

I have been involved with Circles now for more than a decade, working with schools and teachers across the world, mostly in Australia. This revision is based on all I have learnt. After much thought, I have dropped the word 'Time' and added 'Solutions'. Any intervention for social and emotional learning needs to go beyond a timetabled slot in the week to become an integral part of individual, class and whole school development, seeking constructive ways forward for everyday social and emotional issues for everyone (Elias, 2010; Roffey and McCarthy, 2013).

Although it is critical that Circle sessions happen regularly, students need to reflect on and practise what they are learning. When the principles for Circle Solutions (CS), summarized as respect, agency, positivity, inclusion, democracy and safety, are embedded throughout the day and across the school, the desired outcomes are more likely to be sustainable. Seeing Circle sessions as an 'extra' misses the point. Even if someone else facilitates a Circle, the teacher needs to be an active participant to enable and strengthen pupils' understanding and skills.

CS adopts a solution-focused, strengths-based approach. It promotes group agency to encourage young people to take responsibility for themselves and each other. Specific problems and incidents are never discussed in Circles, only issues and directions for change. The focus away from the personal to consideration of topics that impact on young lives make Circles a safer and more comfortable place for both teachers and students. This responds to some of the criticisms and concerns that have been expressed about 'therapeutic education' (Ecclestone and Hayes, 2008) and is congruent with a relational approach to behaviour in school (Roffey, 2011).

What is Wellbeing?

Wellbeing is not simply subjective happiness. Although feeling good about yourself and the world around you is part of wellbeing, it is much more than this. Subjective happiness can be self-absorbed and shallow – based in being successful, rich, attractive and popular. None of this brings sustainable wellbeing. As Wilkinson and Pickett (2010) demonstrate in their analysis of their research on equality, authentic wellbeing begins with 'we'.

In the last decade there has been a welcome move in psychology away from a deficit model, which focuses on diagnosing and treating problems, to exploring what is effective in promoting wellbeing and what helps people to 'flourish' in their lives. Seligman (2011) summarizes this with the acronym PERMA:

- Predominantly **Positive** feelings – about yourself and the world around you.
- **Engagement** – being absorbed by what you are doing – not bored or anxious about performance.
- **Relationships** – having positive interactions with others and managing differences and conflicts well.
- **Meaning and purpose** – living a life that you see as worthwhile.
- **Achievement or Attainment** – setting your own goals and reaching them.

Keyes and Haidt (2003) define flourishing as positive psycho-social functioning. They say this happens when we accept and like most parts of ourselves, see ourselves as developing into better people, have warm and trusting relationships and a degree of self-determination.

The above is congruent with the research on resilience, the factors that enable people to recover from adversities in their lives (Benard, 2004). Protective factors for children include having someone who believes in the best of you, high expectations from those around you and feeling you belong somewhere. Personal factors include a positive outlook and sense of humour, willingness to talk about issues, problem-solving abilities, confidence, determination not to give up too soon – and not being overly gender defined. We need to grow boys who will become 'good men', willing and able to take responsibility for themselves and others rather than fitting a macho image. Girls need to develop the confidence to grasp the opportunities available and be motivated to support each other.

School and Student Wellbeing

Wellbeing is different from welfare or pastoral care in schools. Welfare is a response to individuals who come to the attention of staff because their exceptional needs become apparent. This is usually the province of senior or specialist personnel and requires a specific intervention. A focus on wellbeing by comparison is universal and proactive. Research on student wellbeing (Noble et al., 2008) summarizes the pathways to wellbeing in education. These are: physical and emotional safety, pro-social values, social and emotional learning, a supportive and caring school community, a strengths-based approach, a sense of purpose and a healthy lifestyle. As the MindMatters and KidsMatter mental health initiatives in Australia say: 'Every teacher is a teacher for wellbeing'. The research indicates that such a focus not only helps address mental health issues but also promotes pro-social and ethical behaviour, academic engagement and learning and also teacher wellbeing (Roffey, 2012a). The evidence and rationale for developing wellbeing in schools is overwhelming.

Why We Need Circle Solutions for Wellbeing

Academic achievement opens doors but does not necessarily lead to successful and worthwhile lives or the development of thriving communities. CS aims to promote wellbeing for all students, both the vulnerable and the achieving. This includes healthy relationships, resilience in the face of adversity and responsible behaviour. These three aspects are symbiotic and together lead to more effective learning environments and flourishing individuals.

Many young people today face major challenges. Although poverty is a reality for some, economic disadvantage is not the only adversity children experience. There is less stability and more stress in families, increased mobility as a result of social and political unrest, more mental illness and addiction, high levels of social exclusion and a competitive ethos that categorizes some people as 'losers'. Bullying behaviour and hypocrisy are rife.

The importance of strong communities has been eroded and children may have few good role models to help them learn emotionally literate and considerate behaviour. Teachers now talk about 'bubble-wrapped children', who are over-protected, not allowed to experience anything negative, nor encouraged to become independent. We also have young people under extreme pressure to achieve who may have little chance to be still and reflect on who they are becoming. Children from traditionally 'good' homes who have not learned any coping or problem-solving strategies and are not well connected to others, may go to pieces when faced with failure, loss or other stress.

Where children receive loving, facilitative parenting (Mosco and O'Brien, 2012), which also sets out clear boundaries and high appropriate expectations, children grow up in an optimal environment for their wellbeing. But this is not the case for everyone. For some individuals what happens in schools can make all the difference to their future. Although teachers rarely get acknowledged for this, an educator's belief in the best of a student can change that person's life and future.

CS gives young people a safe space to consider the diverse social and emotional issues that impact on their lives. Structured activities enable children to think through the fundamentals of relationships together with their peers and begin to see there are ways to be in the world that make them feel better about themselves and others.

The Development of Pro-social Behaviour

Effective teachers are in charge of classroom situations – well prepared and able to deliver stimulating lessons. This is different from controlling students. Imposing external discipline does little to change behaviour over the longer term, although students may learn that they must behave in certain ways to keep out of trouble. This puts a focus on what they can get away with rather than helping them understand that it can be worthwhile to be considerate to others, regardless of who is watching. When young people receive the message that they need to be controlled because they can't control themselves, they will look to others to determine their behaviour rather than make pro-social choices for themselves.

Content and Context for Social and Emotional Learning

The twelve dimensions for social and emotional learning (see Appendix 1) have much in common with the CASEL framework: self-awareness; social awareness; self-management and organization; responsible decision-making; and relationship management. It clarifies and extends these components by separating emotional understanding and skills into different dimensions, and places empathy under 'situational' awareness, which includes the importance of timing. It adds dimensions of shared humanity, positivity, ethics and spirituality. There are plenty of socially skilled individuals who do not care much about others, and shared humanity is intended to address this. Goal-setting and confidence comes under leadership. As people can often establish positive interactions but are confounded when relationships present challenges, dealing with conflict is also considered separately. This framework considers contextual issues and looks at what is congruent within an educational setting. CS impacts on whole school processes and interactions – not just what happens in one class in one lesson a week – as the research highlights the importance of contextual factors for sustainable change (Elias et al., 2003).

The Principles of the Circle Solutions Philosophy

The following principles are the foundations of CS – both for the content of Circle sessions and the context in which they are embedded. They can be remembered under the acronym RAPIDS, and perhaps a teacher can think about negotiating the RAPIDS!

Respect
The guidelines emphasize respect for individuals and their contributions. The way we listen to each other matters. As issues may be discussed but not incidents, there is no blaming, naming or shaming. Students who experience respect are more likely to act with respect towards others.

Agency
Everyone is responsible for creating a safe and positive atmosphere. Pupils work together to construct solutions to class issues rather than being told what to do. Giving students agency helps change from an 'external locus of control', where you believe everything just happens to you, to an 'internal locus of control', where you learn that you can effect change.

Positivity
Many activities deliberately foster positive emotions. When people feel better about themselves and others they have more emotional resources to cope with challenges (Fredrickson, 2011). An increased sense of belonging raises resilience. When there is a need to discuss a problem (e.g. bullying, exclusion) this is changed to seeking a solution. What will help us develop a friendly, inclusive, fair and happy classroom for everyone?

Inclusion
Everyone in a class is welcomed into the Circle and students are expected to work with all their classmates. Mixing pupils up so that they get to know each other is a key feature.

Democracy
There are equal opportunities to contribute. No one group or individual is able to dominate. Knowing everyone has their turn promotes cooperation.

Safety and choice
No one is pressured to speak and participants may 'pass' for as long as they like. By being in the Circle they are watching, listening and learning. Pupils usually join in when they have enough confidence or something to say.

The aim for CS is for students to think reflectively and creatively, talk together about important issues, grow to have understanding about themselves and others, and over time to develop knowledge and skills that they can put into practice. The skill lies with the facilitator asking good questions and making the links for students between the activities and the learning.

The Social and Emotional Climate of Classrooms and Schools

A wealth of research now highlights the importance of a caring ethos for both wellbeing and academic outcomes (Cohen, 2006; Horsch et al., 2002; Zins et al., 2004). Schools that have a culture of inclusion and a focus on wellbeing benefit everyone, not only the more vulnerable pupils (Skiba et al., 2006). CS impacts on:

Teacher–student relationships
Many teachers have commented that Circles have both changed the way they see individuals and increased their enjoyment of teaching. Any behaviour management strategy is more effective when implemented by a teacher who has established a positive relationship with a student (Roffey, 2004, 2011).

Reducing bullying
Interventions have moved away from focusing exclusively on students who bully and those who are bullied to a whole school approach. Bullying can only thrive in a culture that either passively or actively condones it. Fear, anxiety, discomfort, anger and disempowerment can thread through a school, undermining positive relationships. Motivating and empowering bystanders to discourage bullying is one of the more promising approaches (Rigby and Bagshaw, 2006). Circles change how students perceive one another and create an ethos where bullying behaviour is challenged.

Developing pro-social behaviour
Reward and sanctions have limited effect in changing behaviour, especially when strong emotions are involved. Circles help individuals explore their emotional reactions in situations. Where students are also given structured opportunities to establish positive relationships with others they have more motivation to behave in pro-social ways.

Mental health and resilience
There are many initiatives to help young people cope with the myriad of difficulties they face in life. These include anger management, peer mediation and social skills programs. Research indicates, however, that all such initiatives need to be integral to the life of the school to maximize sustainability (Murray, 2004). CS is not a stand-alone program but an intervention embedded in school life.

Democracy and citizenship
What happens in schools has an impact on what happens in societies. CS gives all students the opportunity to consider their perspectives and express their opinion. This develops a sense of ownership and responsibility.

Values and human rights
School mission statements often include values such as respect. Circles provide a space for deconstruction of these values, what they mean and why they are important.

Promoting acceptance and reducing prejudice
Intolerance of difference is the basis of much conflict in the world. CS promotes acceptance by breaking down stereotypes and exploring commonalities. Circle activities also celebrate differences and the uniqueness of each individual.

Theoretical Foundations of Circle Solutions

The CS philosophy is based in several ways of thinking about learning, human interaction, wellbeing and the development of pro-social behaviours. The following brief summary is intended to support eclectic practice and guide those who wish to explore these theories more deeply.

Positive Psychology and Solution-focused Approaches

Positive psychology focuses on the study of positive emotions, character strengths and healthy institutions. It researches authentic happiness and wellbeing (e.g. Keyes and Haidt, 2003; Seligman, 2011; Roffey, 2012b). CS helps students identify their diverse strengths and encourages constructive collaboration to deal with everyday issues. An indirect approach focusing on what is wanted can work better than a more direct problem-based approach. Instead of bullying, we talk about safety; instead of discussing stealing, we talk about trust.

Social Learning Theory

Much learning occurs in a social context, including watching and hearing others. Circles provide many opportunities for both active and reflective learning, and support the attention skills necessary to maximize observational learning, advocating that the facilitator models behaviours they want pupils to learn (Bandura, 1986).

Eco-systemic Theory

This theory, originally developed by Urie Bronfenbrenner (1979), emphasizes that there is rarely a linear cause and effect in human relationships and behaviours. Events, the context in which they occur, interpretations and responses, interact in an accumulative and circular way to produce an outcome at any given time. Circles do not happen in isolation. The skills learnt are generalized and reinforced across the school context.

Social Constructionist Theory

This emphasizes the power of language: what people say and the way they say it create 'realities' for their worlds. CS actively changes conversations in order to construct more positive ways of seeing the world. It is also helpful for students to understand that some emotions are socially constructed; we feel proud or embarrassed by what our culture determines (Potter, 1996; Vygotsky, 1978).

Choice Theory

William Glasser (1997) says everyone has a need for love, freedom, power, belonging and fun. He emphasized the importance of schools' exploring ways to meet these needs within a whole school framework. He highlights the importance of respectful relationships and that everyone needs to take responsibility for the choices that they make. CS puts Choice Theory into practice.

Moral Development Theories

There are different theoretical approaches to moral development, with varied emphases on justice, fairness and the 'ethic of care' (Gilligan, 1982; Kohlberg and Turiel, 1971; Noddings, 2002). Being 'good', however, is not simple obedience to authority and conformity to social norms. It involves understanding why we make the choices we do and what is involved in responsibility towards the self and others. Circles provide an opportunity for reflection on these issues, so moral values can be internalized within a sound personal rationale rather than imposed from without. CS motivates students to choose pro-social behaviour whether anyone is watching or not!

Embedding Circle Solutions as a Tool for Wellbeing

Social and emotional learning requires a congruent context where teachers model high levels of emotional literacy with students, colleagues and families. Policies need to be aligned with the focus on wellbeing. Check Appendix 1 to see how your own school measures up.

2

The Circle Solutions Pedagogy: Maximizing Effectiveness

> The chapter introduces factors that promote positive and sustainable outcomes. This includes what happens in a Circle session and the specific processes that make a difference, especially the role of the facilitator. There are suggestions for what to do when students struggle with expectations, adaptations for children with additional needs and/or language difficulties and dealing with sensitive situations.

CS is not a program; it is a teaching approach and framework for group interaction. It can be used with pupils of all ages and across contexts – including in staff meetings, student councils and even parent workshops. Facilitators choose activities that are appropriate to need and circumstances.

Circle Sessions

Regularity

Circle sessions with pupils need to happen *at least* once a week, more often if possible. In my first experience of Circles they took place after recess every day. The school principal told me his entire school ethos was based on these 'Magic Circles'. This frequency is not often feasible with curriculum demands but timetabling Circle sessions helps to ensure they are not jettisoned for other 'priorities'. They take between 20 and 45 minutes, depending on student age and how often they happen. There is little educational benefit in having Circles occasionally as a 'treat'.

There is a clear format in which pupils and teachers take part in a wide range of individual, paired, small group and whole class activities. Many are presented as games, and participants are regularly mixed up so everyone interacts with everyone else.

Guidelines

I once worked in a school where staff told me they had abandoned the language of 'rules' as everything was based on values. I have followed their lead and changed the terminology to Circle 'guidelines'. This may seem minor but words matter. 'Rules' imply an imposition by an external authority, whereas 'guidelines' suggest a consensus in the interests of everyone. There are three basic guidelines based on the principles of democracy, respect, safety and inclusion:

1. Everyone has a turn: when it is your turn to speak, everyone will listen to you – this means you need to listen to others.
2. You may pass if you wish – there is no pressure to say anything.
3. There are no put-downs, either verbal or non-verbal – only personal positives.

Sitting in a Circle

This is both symbolic and practical. In a Circle, no one is isolated or left out. Everyone is at the same level, has the same right to participate and the same responsibility to others. The boundary between teacher and students is weakened, as facilitators are also participants and expected to abide by the same guidelines.

Everyone can see everyone else, making communication easier. Disrespectful behaviours are less likely to occur, and if they do, it becomes obvious to everyone.

In a Circle it is easier to focus attention on what is happening – distractions are less possible and less powerful. The CS framework reduces the chance of a few individuals 'taking over'. This both encourages participation and inhibits domination by powerful factions. The space in the middle of the Circle enables everyone to mingle together or see clearly what is going on.

Setting Up the Circle

Although moving furniture might at first appear challenging, once a routine is established it rarely presents problems. Plan where tables are going to go, who is going to move what to where, and how to put it all back together at the end. Students are usually motivated to help. Some teachers have re-arranged their classroom to accommodate this way of working.

Circles work better on chairs – participants can move about more easily. If children do sit on the floor, so do the facilitators! Circles outside can be fun but quiet voices tend to be blown away by the slightest breeze. The best place for a Circle, if possible, is in the classroom. This helps integrate Circle outcomes with everyday teaching and learning.

Resources

Many activities require little in the way of additional materials. A facilitator would be advised, however, to have a selection of resources available. These might include the following:

- a 'talking stick' to show whose turn it is to speak
- separate emotions on cards: words and/or pictures depending on the age and ability of students
- books, stories, video clips and pictures for use as stimulus material
- strength cards or similar
- rolls of paper and coloured pens

- old cards for cutting up into pieces for getting groups together or for collages
- music, visualizations and reflections
- materials for favourite games.

A list of published and Internet resources is in Appendix 3.

What Happens in a Circle Session?

A Typical Half-hour Circle

Reminder of the guidelines (1 minute)
Introductory game (2 minutes)
Mix-up activity (2 minutes)
Pair share with feedback or paired interviews (2 minutes for pair share, 5 minutes for feedback)
Whole Circle activity or game (5 minutes)
Small group activity or discussion (10 minutes with feedback)
Calming activity to close the Circle (3 minutes).

Each Circle session is different. Although the content is flexible, the principles are consistent.

Reminder of the Guidelines

Once everyone is in the Circle there is a statement of the guidelines by either the teacher or students:

- everyone has a turn and when one person is talking everyone else listens
- you do not have to say anything; you may pass
- there are no put-downs – only personal positives.

An Introductory Game

This can be a greeting, name game, check-in or sentence completion. This ensures everyone has the chance to participate at the outset but keeps contributions brief. It helps students feel they are being 'heard' and supports listening skills. For sentence completions give everyone a moment to think of what they will say. A check-in could be as simple as a thumbs up/thumbs down for how things are going today, or a sentence completion such as 'Since the last Circle ...'. The facilitator will often go first to model what is expected.

Mix-up Activity

Mixing up is an essential feature of Circles as it provides opportunities for individuals to interact with others outside of their usual social network. It happens several times a session but especially before paired activities. Silent statements also mix people up.

Activities with a Partner

Pair Share with Feedback
This is a structured conversation seeking commonalities. Ask for two items so each person says one each in feedback.

Paired Interviews
Each partner finds out something specific about the other, promoting asking and listening. If there will be feedback, each person is asked what may be shared with the whole Circle to demonstrate an important element of respect. Partners may need to be reminded to swap around.

Whole Circle Activity or Game

This is where students have most fun and is a great motivator, especially when Circles are being introduced.

Small Group Activity or Discussion

Small group work is particularly valuable for collaborative activities and for identifying solutions to issues, such as inclusion. Brief feedback to the whole group may be recorded if these are strategies to address whole-class issues. Stimulus material such as stories, pictures, music or film clips can be useful.

Calming Closing Activity

Here students can learn relaxation techniques, develop visualization, mindfulness, meditative skills or just reflect on their learning. If the Circle has been lively it provides a calm space before a return to more academic activities.

Planning Circle Sessions

It is useful to have a general idea of what you want to address throughout the year, but be prepared to do this flexibly. Work with issues most relevant to your class and follow student lead when appropriate. Usually it will be clear what needs addressing:

> Children knew little about their feelings and how to regulate emotions. They acted on impulse rather than logic, and lacked assertive skills. There were deficiencies in communication and little awareness of or relationships with others. (Student facilitator in McCarthy, 2009)

After just ten weeks of Circles there was evidence of change:

> It was remarkable to see the children I had been working with since March working together as a team and creating friendships and bonds ... no longer were they being disruptive and not talking to one another.

Establish familiarity with positive Circles in the first few weeks. Students will not engage with more challenging topics until they feel safe with the teacher and each other. Use the third person rather than ask for personal contributions until trust has been established and never address incidents directly in Circles as this increases the potential for blame. Identify the issues that arise from incidents and work with these. For example, one high school had an incident of racism and addressed issues of inclusion, fairness and 'shared humanity' rather than deconstruct exactly what happened. This approach delivers more sustainable solutions as issues can be revisited over time and in different ways.

It is often possible to use a curriculum or other priority area on which to structure activities. This might include personal, social and health education, citizenship education, safe schools frameworks that address bullying, values, leadership programs or positive behaviour lessons.

The Importance of Process: What You Need to Make Circles Work

Students are usually highly motivated once they realize how enjoyable Circles can be. Unless there are really exceptional circumstances, Circles need to be maintained as part of the class routine. Teachers say it can take up to four weeks to establish familiarity with the Circle framework so persevere if things don't go to plan straight away.

Although this book contains many ideas to choose from there are numerous other resources available. Sometimes students will create their own games or bring in new ideas from home. Stimulus materials can be helpful. Stories, pictures and video clips enable students to discuss emotions and difficult issues without referring to themselves. Asking young people to discuss 'What might someone your age think or do?' can help create psychological distance and safety.

You know that Circles are being really effective when you see changes in students at other times in the school day. The following are comments from teachers:

> One kid will say, 'I get lonely in the playground sometimes' and people who have never seen this kid before will say 'Oh well, I'll be with you at lunchtime if you like.'

> I found that the whole positive rephrasing, not using 'put-downs', has rolled over into every day.

And, from a student:

> You think about when you've done bad things and you want to make up for it.

Students may welcome acknowledgement for the changes to develop a positive, supportive class – it is *their* ideas and actions making a difference.

Why Games?

Children today no longer routinely play out in the street and are rarely allowed in parks without the watchful eye of an adult. Privileged pupils may spend their lives being ferried from one activity to another. Less advantaged children may live in an increasingly passive world where they watch others do things on TV. Games often mean solitary computer games or competitive sports where winning is all that matters.

Games for Circle sessions are not individually competitive (though teams may compete) and aim to promote both inclusion and a range of positive feelings and reflections. It is not surprising that Circles are such an engaging pedagogy. Play is a much more important part of human development than is often acknowledged – and it doesn't stop when you are 5 years old (Roffey and Hromek, 2009).

Getting Circles Started

For some pupils the Circle pedagogy is a different way of learning. Most take to it immediately with great enthusiasm. Others take time to get used to having a voice, being given choices and being asked to respect and listen to others. The facilitator takes part in *all* activities. This promotes confidence and shows students what to do. Give students time to consider the guidelines and what they mean.

The Guidelines

When one person is speaking everyone else listens
Many Circle facilitators have incorporated a physical symbol – a 'talking piece' or 'talking stick' – that indicates whose turn it is to speak. This is especially useful for it reinforces the principle of equality in the Circle:

- everyone sees whose turn it is to speak
- it encourages thinking before speaking
- it encourages the contribution of quieter students
- it increases peer pressure to listen.

No put-downs: personal positives only
Defining what this means may take several sessions. A sentence completion activity can help:

- A put-down would be …
- Someone would feel put down in a Circle if …
- A put-down would feel …
- Our Circles need to be …
- Personal positives could include …
- A personal positive needs to be …
- Getting a genuine compliment would make someone feel …

Another helpful activity is to ask your students to interview one another about what a put-down is and how it makes them feel about themselves and the person who does it. Then ask them to talk about personal positives in the same way.

As Circles address issues not incidents, there is less opportunity for blame.

You may pass
Some students pass all the time at first. Smile and nod to acknowledge this is acceptable. You may wish to ask everyone at the end of the activity if they have now thought of something, but do not ask individuals – it puts them on the spot and may make them anxious.

Teachers sometimes find it difficult to accept that pupils choose not to contribute, especially if there are several in a class. Remember they are still listening, watching and learning from others and this is a legitimate way of gaining knowledge and skills. Usually they will take part in the whole group and non-verbal activities. Evidence indicates that all students eventually choose to speak when they feel sufficiently confident and comfortable, though this may take longer for some.

Even when students appear to use the pass rule as defiance, this can be interpreted as not yet feeling safe enough to participate fully. Sometimes pupils get into a routine of repeating what someone else has just said. This stops in time and individuals become more creative and innovative in their contributions.

On-going Monitoring and Evaluation

This not only helps the teacher know how Circles are going, but also supports those students who want it to go well but might be 'shouted down' by a powerful and negative minority. This can be done in several ways:

Sentence completion

- The best thing about Circles is ...
- Circles make our class a better place to be because ...

Small group discussions

- The games we like most
- The best things we have learnt from Circles
- Three things that would make Circles even better
- Our responsibilities in Circles

The Role of the Circle Facilitator

The way in which Circles are run is central to their effectiveness, and the skills of the facilitator are critical. Sometimes teachers take too much control, do not themselves abide by the guidelines or make few links with learning. This section ensures that Circles are facilitated appropriately, with skill and sensitivity.

Facilitator participation
This is no time to 'stand and deliver!' Teachers sit in the Circle with students and only stand when an activity demands this. They participate in all activities, often going first to show pupils what to do and encourage others to join in.

Facilitator modelling
They show what is expected by conforming to the CS principles and guidelines. This means listening respectfully to all contributions and not putting anyone down. This is particularly important when dealing with students who struggle or are disruptive (see later in this chapter for detailed responses).

Facilitator attitude
Expectations are self-fulfilling. Facilitators need to believe that relationships are relevant to the learning environment and that students can learn skills that will benefit both individuals and the whole class. Where facilitators are positive and

optimistic, maintain high expectations of their students and expect Circles to work well, this is more likely to happen.

Choosing activities
Activities need to be mostly short, not too complicated and enjoyable. Some may take place over more than one session. Although there are few opportunities for self-disclosure, teachers need to be sensitive to their class and the needs of individuals to ensure that Circles remain safe.

Being flexible
Sometimes an activity does not seem to be working well for some reason. Be prepared to bring this to a close or try a change of pace.

Introducing activities
Choose initial activities that are motivating and simple to understand; if necessary, break down instructions into small manageable chunks and demonstrate. Games where students get to know each other and fun mix-up activities are particularly good. Facilitator enthusiasm is critical. Even the best games can fall flat with a half-hearted introduction. Make sure everyone has a turn quickly. If students are unsure what to do they need the opportunity to ask questions. If a group is not doing as asked, the facilitator needs to take responsibility for any confusion and give instructions again. It is useful modelling to be able to admit a mistake, however small.

Making links between activities and learning
Every activity has a learning outcome. Skilled facilitation includes making a brief link with what is being learnt about resilience, relationships or classroom ethos. Even where the activity is just about having fun, it helps students to realize that they can have fun in safe and supportive ways. It is just as important to make links between what is learnt in Circle sessions and what happens in the class at other times. Ask students to reflect back if an issue arises. Visible reminders in the classroom will help.

Maintaining pace
Ensure pupils have opportunities to move about – no Circle session should be all sitting. Energizers help maintain a good pace. Individual activities may be limited in larger classes, especially for younger children. Sometimes time restrictions make it difficult for everyone to give feedback from a small group, so one student may be nominated to do this. Give others a chance to comment.

Keeping on track
As well as the strategies described below for trouble-shooting, 'I' statements are helpful. 'I need one person to speak at a time so I can hear what is being said' is easier to hear than: 'Stop talking all at once'. Using a visual cue to get attention can be invaluable – (see 'Transition' in Chapter 3).

Treating everyone equally
Thank everyone for each contribution, giving a smile, brief positive comment or nod – even if the contribution is less than what is required. The student will know it isn't; you don't have to say.

Giving students opportunities to take a lead

You will notice that 'teacher' and 'facilitator' are used interchangeably but activities may have a 'leader'. As students become familiar with the Circle framework encourage them to design, develop and present activities. This promotes agency and responsibility.

Maintaining a focus on inclusion

This principle of Circle Solutions is critical to addressing the needs of more vulnerable and often challenging students. It is also often the issue of most concern to teachers. The aim is to use the framework itself to determine teacher responses (see below).

Running Circles can change the relationships between teachers and students. One teacher told me that she thought that a pupil 'had it in for me', imagining that he lay awake at night plotting! After the class had been doing Circles for a few weeks she 'realized that his behaviour had nothing to do with me; I began to see him differently and relate to him more positively. Over time his behaviour improved.'

Inclusion and Troubleshooting

One of the principles of Circle Solutions is inclusion. Students with the greatest difficulties probably need the learning and support provided in Circles more than anyone. Responses to challenging issues need to be thought through so the facilitator continues to abide by the principles but also ensures that Circles are positive for all. It is a tricky balance but an important one. It can be summed up as giving chances and choices while maintaining high expectations. Abiding by the Circle guidelines is critical – other behaviours such as inappropriate sitting are irritating but not necessarily relevant. When the facilitator focuses on the CS principles they are not using up valuable time and energy on a multitude of other potential misdemeanours.

Students Who 'Muck Up'

Try these strategies in sequence. We often take strong action too early and are left with nothing in reserve!

At the outset

- Ignore minor silliness or inappropriate comments. Children usually do this for attention – it is rewarding for you to give it, however negative.
- Use proximity praise – giving attention to those who are behaving as required, especially if they are sitting near to the one who isn't, e.g. 'thank you, Dillon and Leo, for listening'. If the pupil begins to conform, thank them also – giving the attention they need but for wanted behaviour.
- Stop the activity and say: 'We are just going to wait until everyone is ready.'
- Stop the activity and repeat the guidelines to everyone, so no student or group is singled out.
- If necessary, repeat this last strategy several times. It is surprisingly effective.
- Introduce a mix-up activity that breaks up disruptive groups. You may need to have a few activities planned so students do not return to the same place.

On-going individual difficulties

- If you have a student still behaving in an unacceptable way, introduce a paired or small group activity for everyone else and use the opportunity to speak with them privately.
- Begin by saying they are important in the Circle and you want them to be there.
- Then say: to stay in the Circle they will need to abide by the guidelines.
- Ask what they want to do.
- If they choose to stay in the Circle tell them how pleased you are they have made this decision. You might ask what might help them keep on track.
- If they re-join the Circle and their behaviour improves, commend them privately at the end of the session.
- If they choose to stay out tell them that they are always welcome to come back again so long as they abide by the guidelines. It is always their choice. Find the student some work to do.
- When the next Circle takes place comment positively if they begin to join in or ask them what they have decided to do today.
- If a student re-joins but is unable to conform, you again take them quietly to one side and ask them to sit out for this activity and come back for the next if they feel they are able to do so.
- Occasionally students continue to disrupt from outside. Special arrangements may need to be made for such individuals, but they need to know that they will be welcomed back into the Circle whenever they think they can manage this. Asking students if they would like to join in for the last 5 minutes and then increasing that time might help.

You may have a student with particular social or emotional needs that make it hard for them to conform. One strategy is to provide things for them to do at a table just outside the Circle and let them join in with activities of their choice. When in the Circle this pupil has to conform to the guidelines like everyone else.

One teacher found that very short, fun Circles that got gradually longer were successful in accommodating a seriously traumatized child.

Group Difficulties

Sometimes several students muck up and make it difficult for Circles to run smoothly. In the first instance, put the issue back to the Circle.

Silent statements show how much students have in common:

- Stand up and change places if you enjoy being in Circles sometimes.
- Stand up and change places if you enjoy lots of Circle activities.
- Stand up and change places if you would like Circles to continue.

Pair share and feedback on two activities both enjoyed.

Small group activities

- Ask what should happen to make Circles more enjoyable for everyone.
- Ask groups to plan a perfect Circle.
- Ask groups to plan and then run a Circle for everyone on a theme of their choice.

Other ideas

An outline of the Circle session on the board with an option to change an activity increases commitment.

When students find it difficult to calm down after a session it makes sense to have Circles at the end of the day.

Focusing on small group activities rather than whole Circle games might also help.

One teacher analysed why her class was resistant to Circles and found that not having tables made them feel exposed and vulnerable. She moved sessions outside for a while, where students stood rather than sat and played 'sporty' non-verbal games. The talking component was gradually reintroduced with non-threatening topics, then mix-up games and fun collaborative activities. It took a term to get the class back inside with a traditional Circle format but eventually this happened.

Another teacher asked students to come up with suggestions to help those who could not conform so that they could all have a good time.

Persistence and involving students usually pays off. If the Circle is lively most students will not want to miss out on the fun and will have a vested interest in it continuing; the more serious stuff can come later.

Younger children sometimes respond positively to the teacher using a puppet as the Circle 'facilitator'.

Encouraging students to take turns in leading some structured activities may increase confidence in shyer individuals and provide opportunities for students who are dominant to use their abilities more constructively.

In the last resort, run voluntary Circles. This could be during class time while others work (probably harder to organize) or at break time.

Some teachers have divided larger class groups to make Circles more manageable. You will not get all the benefits of developing a whole class ethos, but it may be a temporary solution.

Students with Learning Difficulties

Circles cater for many different learning styles – visual, auditory, kinaesthetic, experiential, individual and cooperative – so there is something for everyone. Circles are not overly dependent on academic skills and therefore are usually suitable for a wide ability range. You may wish, however, to have activities at the beginning of the Circle that include everyone and then do one or more of the following:

- Ask a small group to support a particular child so they are always part of what is going on – this should not always be the same people, so everyone gets a chance to be a supporter.
- Amend more challenging activities so that there is a specific role for an individual which they can manage.

Students with Language Difficulties

Circles offer an excellent place to develop language skills, as they support development in a structured way. Many non-verbal activities ensure everyone is included. Students who have less fluent language than others may need more opportunities to watch and listen rather than actively participate. They need to be aware of the 'pass rule' so they feel safe at all times.

Increase participation for children with language difficulties by maximizing visual support: give them models to copy, pictures to reinforce words and alternative communication strategies such as miming or drawing. Limit the amount of language given at any one time, speak slowly and use simple terms supported by gestures and expressions. Where students are learning English as an additional language, more fluent students may be paired with them. This needs to be planned so the responsibility is shared. Other languages and signing might be introduced where children learn songs from other countries or how to use simple signs to aid communication.

Students with hearing impairment are more able to see faces in Circles and can therefore lip-read more easily.

Sensitive Issues and Confidentiality

Circles focus primarily on strengths and positives, but there will be times when discussions touch on harsh realities in students' lives. The Circle is safer when the group stays with general issues and the third person, rather than asking for personal information. Activities in this revised edition limit the use of the word 'I' for this reason.

Prevent

Many classes have their own guidelines for Circles including: 'What is said in the Circle, stays in the Circle'. This can be problematic as some information does have to be taken further, and if parents enquire students might say 'I mustn't tell you', which does little for trust in school–family relationships. It can be helpful to remind pupils that they take responsibility for what they choose to say and can speak only for themselves. If young people gossip about what has been said in damaging or hurtful ways, this needs to become an issue that everyone addresses.

Pre-empt

Let students know that if an activity makes them feel uncomfortable they may step out of the Circle and do something else on their own. Re-emphasize the 'pass' guideline. If a facilitator realizes that a student is disclosing very personal information then gentle intervention would be appropriate. It is vital that this is done by giving the impression that what they are saying is too important for Circle rather than dismissing it. They may be encouraged to speak afterwards with the teacher and perhaps to write or draw about it.

Protect

If there is someone in school who takes responsibility for listening to students then it may be appropriate to refer to them. Disclosures that indicate serious harm require mandatory reporting. All students should be aware that this is the case, whether in Circles, a counselling session or an informal conversation with a teacher.

Embedding Circle Solutions as a Tool for Wellbeing

Evidence suggests that the CS pedagogy is engaging and motivating for students (Roffey and McCarthy, 2013). Are there ways you might generalize some of these strategies – such as cooperative learning – into other areas of the curriculum?

Using CS principles to respond to unwanted behaviour is also often effective. Could you adopt similar techniques in other situations or use these strategies to promote more positive behaviour in general?

3

The Basics

In this chapter you will find a wide range of activities for opening a Circle session, managing the transition from one activity to another, mixing participants up, energizers for when things feel a bit flat, and calming, closing activities. Unless otherwise indicated, activities are appropriate for all ages.

It is useful for all students to have a CS file where they can collect things about themselves and record more personal and/or difficult issues. Some have developed a reflective Circle journal to keep track of their learning and development.

Opening and Greetings

All Circle sessions begin with a reminder of the guidelines, either given by the teacher or students:

- when one person is speaking everyone listens
- there are no put-downs
- you may pass.

Silent Greetings

For the following activities, one person carries out the action towards the person sitting on their left or right. This goes around the Circle until it reaches the person it started with. For all early Circle sessions the facilitator would go first.

- Pass the smile
- High five
- Handshake
- Mexican wave – everyone stands up in turn and throws their arms in the air and sits down again, perhaps calling out their name. There are many variations for this – ask students to think of some.
- Pass the wink

- Pass the squeeze – once the class can do this smoothly, you can add sound. When the squeeze is going to the left you say 'Ooh', and when it is going to the right you say 'Aahh'. Send a couple of squeezes around, speed it up and place people as 'stations' where the squeeze can change direction.

Spoken Greetings

- My name is …
- Introduce the person on your right, say your own name and then introduce the person on your left.
- Go around the Circle with as many different greetings you can think of: 'Hi', 'Hello', 'Good morning', 'Nice to see you', 'How's it going?'
- I am [positive adjective] name: 'I am daring Danni', 'I am happy Harry', 'I am marvellous Mustapha'.
- Introduce yourself with a statement that begins with the same letter as your name. This can be phrased as 'I like … ', or 'I can …': 'I am Kristen and I like karaoke'. 'I am Timmy and I can touch my toes'.

Hello Goodbye

The class wander around the centre of the Circle. At a given signal they have to say a greeting word to the person nearest to them. If both say the same greeting they are 'out' and sit down in the Circle. The game continues either until everyone is sitting down or at a time limit. Now play the game with words for 'goodbye'.

Variations

Teach various greetings for different cultures:

- In Paris they kiss four times on alternate cheeks.
- In Russia they give a bear hug.
- Germans have a strong handshake with a hand on the arm as well.
- The Japanese put their hands together at chest level and bow from the waist.
- Thai people put their hands together at forehead level and bow their head.
- The Spanish and Portuguese kiss on alternate cheeks.
- The British often give a simple handshake.
- The Americans give a 'high five' if they know each other well.
- Maoris and the Inuit rub noses.
- Australians slap each other on the back with a smile.

Get everyone to move around and, at the whistle, the leader shouts out a country. Pairs greet each other in the appropriate way.

Half the class represents one country, and the other half another country.

Extension Discussions

How does it feel when you meet someone from another culture who offers a different greeting from you?

What must it be like for those who are in a different country?

Check-in   YMS

To show how they are doing today each person shows a thumbs up or down (or in the middle) or places their hand on an imaginary bar in front of them from the floor to as high as they can reach.

Sentence Completion

- Since the last Circle ...

Name Games: Combined Words and Actions

Stand and sit again as you say your name or when it is spoken by others.

Soft Balls   YMS

Everyone stands in a close Circle. One person says their own name and then the name of the person they throw the ball to. This person repeats the action and puts their hands behind their back to show they have had a turn. When everyone has been named, reverse the sequence so everyone throws the ball back to the person who threw it to them. Remind pupils to remember who this was.

Variations

When you drop a ball you play with a 'forfeit', for example, use one hand only then go down on one knee. You can 'regain' this loss with a subsequent catch so the aim is for others to help you out and get you back on your feet again.

With music: the aim is to not be holding the ball when the music stops.

Bunnies   YMS

The game begins with someone putting both hands up on their head as 'bunny ears', waggling their fingers. The person on their right puts up their left hand as an ear; the person on their left puts up their right hand. The middle person 'passes the bunny' by calling out the name of another person in the circle and pointing at them with both their hands. This person becomes the 'bunny' with those on either side also putting up the nearest hand. This is a great game for concentration, especially for those on either side of the bunny. Continue until everyone has had a turn. When you have had a turn you sit on your hands (on your bunny ears). You can also play this as a 'silent' game without names.

Names on a Train

A student volunteers to be the train conductor. They go up to someone in the Circle and say: 'What's your name?' When they say their name, e.g. 'Jack', the conductor says 'come on board, Jack'. Jack then goes to the front of the train and approaches another in the Circle, asking: 'What's your name?' He repeats the name, the 'conductor' behind him repeats the name and says 'come on board, ... '. This game continues with each successive person coming onto the front of the train. Names travel down the line until they reach the 'conductor' at the back who welcomes them 'on board'. When the last person has been picked up the conductor calls: 'Everybody off the train', and everyone goes back to a chair in the Circle. Students can lift their arms up and down or make train noises as they go around the Circle 'picking up passengers' to add to the energy.

Chaser

One student is sent outside while the class identifies someone to be the Chaser. The student returns and walks around the outside of the Circle tapping gently on each person's head. As each person is tapped they say their name loudly. When the Chaser is tapped they call out 'Chaser!' – and try to catch the student before they reach the empty seat. Do this enough times for everyone to call out their name.

Autographs

Everyone has a copy of the class roll to take around to each of their classmates. Everyone signs next to their name. You could ask how their name is pronounced if it is unusual, or whether they prefer to be known by a shortened version or nickname. Each individual therefore has a brief interaction with everyone in the class.

Why My Name?

Names are an important part of our identity.

In pairs, students interview their partner about their name. Where did it come from? Is there anything special or unusual about it? Do they like it? Students introduce their partners to the Circle. Give students some notice before this activity so they can ask their families.

Transitions

After a paired or small group activity the facilitator needs to regain everyone's attention. The best way to do this is to negotiate it with the Circle. Here are a few you might like to suggest or try:

- clapping rhythm and then hands on knees – everyone copies
- fingers on noses – everyone follows suit and looks at the teacher
- hand in the air – as above
- folded arms, or hands in laps – as above
- pass the message quietly round the circle
- counting down from five – as people hear the facilitator count they join in, and when everyone gets to one then there is silence
- a small tinkling bell, hooter or other sound.

If students are involved in an intensive small group activity or discussion it is good practice to give warning that time is nearly up. If feedback is required, ask groups to decide who is going to say what. If one person is nominated, others should have the opportunity to add something if they wish.

Mixing Up

Mixing individuals up so they interact with everyone else supports the CS philosophy of inclusion. Students quickly get used to working with a wide range of classmates and although you may get initial objections, this is something students like best about Circles. Mixing up can be done in many different ways.

Personal Categories

Have categories that are as innocuous as possible and do not highlight differences in a potentially hurtful way. What is comfortable would depend on the circumstances of people in the class. These are some examples:
Stand up and change places:

- everyone who has brown eyes (blue, green, grey)
- everyone who has a dog (a brother, sister, a cat)
- everyone who likes bananas (chocolate, spaghetti, orange juice)
- everyone who can swim (climb a tree, whistle a tune, ride a bike)
- everyone with a birthday in …
- everyone who has broken their arm (had chicken pox, had a tooth out)
- everyone whose name begins with (ends with, includes …).

Given Categories

Here the facilitator gives categories to everyone in the Circle, then asks everyone whose category is called to swap places. There are many possibilities. The simplest is to give everyone a number: then you could ring the changes – all even numbers change places, (specific) numbers change places, all numbers that are in the five times table change places. Other categories could be:

- seasons, months, colours, shapes, types of cake, planets, cars, countries, flowers, trees, animals.

Students pair up with new partners as they will be sitting in different places.

Mixing Up Games to Form Small Groups or Find Partners

- Cut up paint-sample cards so that groups find those with the same colour.
- Cut up old greeting or postcards into as many pieces as you need in a group – usually four or five. Jumble the pieces up and give one to each student. They find their group by putting the pieces together.
- Put names or pictures of animals on to cards. Four cards are the same: dog, rabbit, elephant, cat, fish and penguin are good ones. The leader gives each person a card – they memorize it and give it back. They then find the rest of their animal 'family' using only animal noises and actions. You could also put the names of musical instruments, swimming strokes, feelings, sporting teams.
- Find your family – for groups of five. Each person is given a paper with 'Mr', 'Mrs', 'Brother', 'Sister' or 'Baby' and the family name (or variations on this – grandma, mum, daughter, cat and dog – the important thing is the family name at the end). This paper is folded in half. Everyone mingles in the middle, passing on their paper as many times as possible. When the leader calls out 'Find your Family', everyone looks at the paper they now have and seeks others in the same family. You could ask students to do this without words or to line up in a certain order.
- Think of things that go together, such as knife and fork, Batman and Robin, hat and coat or phrases such as 'Happy birthday' or 'Good morning'. Put half of each pair on a card and give the cards out. Students find their 'pair'.
- Half the cards have capital letters and the other half lower case. Students find their matching half.
- Words with two syllables: mon-key, bis-cuit, din-ner, sun-set, light-ning, bas-ket, moun-tain. Pictures on the other side help those who are not yet able to read.

Energizers

These are activities that involve physical action for many in the Circle and as such lift energy levels. There are more energizers in other chapters.

The Warm Wind Blows   YMS

This is also a great game for mixing students up. One chair is removed from the Circle. The leader stands in the middle and says: 'The warm wind blows for everyone who …' and chooses a category that applies to them, and that many others will share. Students change places (including the leader), leaving one person without a chair. They become the leader and choose the next category saying the same phrase. No one can have more than one turn. If someone ends up in the middle for a second time they choose someone who has not had a turn. Categories that many share might be:

- had toast for breakfast
- is wearing white socks
- has long hair
- has ever been camping.

Sea, Shore and Sharks

The leader indicates a line in the middle of the Circle, on one side of which is the shore and on the other is the sea. The leader calls out 'In the sea' or 'On the shore' and the children run to whichever side of the line is the right one and mime whatever they would be doing on a beach or in the water. When the leader calls out 'Sharks!' everyone runs back to a seat in the Circle. You can develop this game by removing one chair so that the person left without a seat is 'out' or becomes the next leader.

Stand Up, Turn Round, Sit Down Stories

Give everyone a part in a short story. This can be either a character or an object. With a large class some students might do this in groups, e.g. you can have several beans in *Jack and the Beanstalk* or several mice in *Cinderella*. When someone hears the name of their part they stand up, turn around and sit down again. Stories need to be suitable for the age and interest of the participants and short enough to hold interest. You may like to give your most energetic students the characters mentioned most!

Closing the Circle

The final activity in a Circle session offers not only a space for students to become calm, but also to reflect on their learning and develop relaxation and mindfulness techniques. Here are some possibilities.

Releasing pressure

Ask students to place their fingers on each side of their head, just above the side of the eyebrow. Make circular movements for a few moments – now move the fingers up and behind the ears, down the neck and finally grasp the shoulders, pressing gently into the back

Tracing letters

Pupils all turn to the right so that they are facing the back of the person next to them. Then they gently trace a letter of the alphabet on that person's upper back, who tries to identify what it is. This is in fact a form of massage and reduces stress.

Mindful Breathing

It is useful to teach students to breathe evenly. This reduces stress and increases calm. Ask everyone to sit comfortably with feet on the floor and hands resting in laps. Students concentrate on their breathing and take a few normal deep breaths. Ask them

(Continued)

(Continued)

to breathe out until their lungs are empty and then breathe in slowly for a count of six so their lungs are expanded, hold the breath in and then breathe out for a count of six. Do this several times. Ask pupils to imagine that each breath fills them with positive energy that passes into their bloodstream and then to all parts of their body.

Who's in Charge?

Read the following slowly to students:

Tell your body to sit (or lie) still. Now tell it to raise one arm, stretch this to the ceiling, now tell it to wiggle the fingers. Now lower that arm and raise the other one. Stretch to the ceiling, wiggle your fingers. Lower that arm. Lift one knee, put it down, lift the other knee, put it down. Move your head to the left side, back to the front, now to the right side. Take a really deep breath, in and out. Now sit and listen to your heart beating and imagine how your heart is pumping blood all around your body. Now listen to your breathing and imagine how your lungs are filling with air and passing oxygen to your blood. Imagine how your stomach is turning food into energy just for you. Think of all the things that make your body so wonderful, all the things that keep your body working well, all the different ways you can be in charge of your body.

Tense and Release

Participants tighten muscles in different parts of their body and then release them. You can do this in different parts of the body separately or start with the feet and work up and then release gradually, so that everything becomes very floppy, the head resting on the chest and arms hanging loosely. Hold this very loose position for a minute.

Sounds   YMS

Everyone sits comfortably, closing their eyes if they wish. Begin by raising awareness of sounds outside of the room, then listen for any sounds in the room. Finally pupils focus on sounds inside themselves, their own breathing and even heartbeat. Do not worry if you get a tummy rumble: a good laugh is relaxing too.

Stretching   YMS

Students stand with feet slightly apart. They begin by reaching with both arms over their head. Bring their arms down level with shoulders but then reach out far in front. Now come down and bend from the waist, trying to touch the floor without bending

(Continued)

(Continued)

the knees. Now ask them to stand sideways so they are facing the back of the person in front. Ask them to stretch as if they are trying to touch the walls on either side. Now they face the front again and this time go very loose and shake out their hands and arms.

Stories/Music

A short story or poem with a gentle theme, a calm piece of music or the sound of the sea or birdsong helps conclude the Circle and helps students leave with a calm, positive feeling.

Visualizations/Imaginations

Visualizations are powerful and when done regularly can have an impact on improving performance. Thoughts can change brain structure. Young people often respond well to the idea that they can create imaginary worlds and enjoy being guided in this. Keep visualizations short enough to maintain concentration for the specific age group. Bring students out of the visualization slowly. Ask pupils to sit comfortably with their feet on the floor, hands in their lap and eyes closed if they wish. Ask them to imagine:

- a friendly place – who is there, what sounds do you hear, what do you notice?
- a safe place – what is in your safe place, how comfortable does it feel, who helps make this safe?
- a magic place – what can you see, what happens there?
- taking a journey.

Sleeping Lions

All students lie on the floor. They stay very still as if they were 'sleeping lions'. When the leader sees someone moving they tap them gently and say which part they saw moving. That student then quietly finds a seat back in the Circle. Students who are 'out' can help the leader by pointing to someone who is wriggling but must stay silent. When there are only a few left on the floor, the leader says 'lions alive' and these children jump and join the Circle.

Affirmations

Students often find it difficult to say positive things about themselves so this activity can be quite powerful. Either have a selection of affirmations from which students choose or give them out randomly. It doesn't matter if you have several of the same. Affirmations are aspirational – they are about becoming as well as being. Here are some examples:

(Continued)

(Continued)

- I am learning to be a good friend.
- I am a lovable person.
- I can be strong in many different ways.
- I am worthy of respect.
- I can learn from mistakes.

When everyone has read out their affirmation ask the Circle to sit quietly for a moment so each person can think about what their affirmation means for them.

Pick a Picture   MS

You can get free postcards from cafes, museums, theatres and art galleries advertising shows, exhibitions, books or organizations. Other pictures or photographs can also be used for this activity.

Scatter a selection of cards/pictures on the floor in the middle of the Circle. Ask students to pick a card that represents one of the following:

- What they learnt from today's Circle
- What they learnt about their class
- What they learnt about (the theme of the Circle)
- The best feeling they had today

Each student says briefly why they chose their particular card – remember they can pass if they wish.

Embedding Circle Solutions as a Tool for Wellbeing

Can you encourage students to work with each other in different groupings during lessons?

How can you reinforce students' knowledge of each other?

Which transition activities suggested here might be useful every day?

Can relaxation activities be built into other times of the day?

Ask students to choose an affirmation a week and practise saying it in front of the mirror at home. Ask if this makes a difference to how they think and feel about themselves, to what they do and what they hope for.

4

Strengths, Dreams and Values

This chapter helps students seek, acknowledge and develop the positive in themselves for now and the future. Alongside awareness of strengths is an understanding of values. Just accepting what is handed down from those in authority impedes the development of a healthy identity. Circle activities here help young people reflect on their strengths and values and how these fit in with their dreams for the future.

Some young people have low self-worth. They believe they cannot do very much or be successful and sometimes feel they are not liked, loved or valued. This may be an outcome of hearing negative things about themselves for many years. When children are constantly told they are 'naughty', 'lazy' or 'a nuisance' this impacts on their self-concept. They may seek ways to feel better by putting others down or just reinforce this negativity by living up to these expectations (MacLure et al., 2012). If they begin to understand that they can be 'helpful', 'resilient' or 'creative', what this means, and that it gains approval, they will begin to develop an alternative self-concept to live up to.

Sometimes students do not find it easy to find anything positive to say about themselves and do not believe it when others do. We need to enable students to think about strengths in the abstract, de-construct what they mean and ensure they know that you do not necessarily *have* a particular quality or ability – but may be in the process of *developing* this. Unrecognized or emerging strengths can be a useful concept. We need to support young people in their 'becoming' the person they choose to be and to help them make good choices for themselves and their communities.

There are now many resources for working with a strengths-based approach – including different kinds of strengths cards. See Appendix 3 for more information.

Strengths

A starter list of strengths is given here. Add to this list as ideas come to you.

Table 4.1   Starter list of strengths

Interpersonal Strengths	Resilience Strengths	Ethical Strengths	Personal Strengths	Ability Strengths
friendly	thankful	responsible	creative	sporting
willing to share	optimistic	honest	adventurous	musical
warm	keeps things in perspective	trustworthy	hard-working	artistic
caring	determined	fair	neat and tidy	imaginative
good listener	cheerful	acknowledges mistakes	sense of humour	can dance
helpful	sets goals	willing to make amends	energetic	good with animals
supportive	adaptable	respects confidentiality	enthusiastic	relaxed
fun to be with	inclusive	reliable	graceful	can fix things
considerate	can change	democratic	generous spirit	colourful
interested	positive	asks questions	courageous	independent
kind	assertive	forgiving	careful	has IT skills
empathic	problem solver	non judgemental	curious	organized, plans ahead
team player	confident	thoughtful	appreciative/ mindful	good communicator
gives compliments	learns from mistakes	makes careful decisions	takes initiative	can make things

Photocopiable:
Circle Solutions for Student Wellbeing © Sue Roffey, 2014 (SAGE)

Silent Statements

Change places if:

- you know something you are good at
- you are taller/stronger than last year
- you know more things than last year
- you enjoy learning about other people in this class
- you can think of a strength you would like to have
- you know someone you look up to and admire
- you believe we can all change.

Activities with a Partner

Pair share followed by sentence completion – you can use this for all strengths:

- Being reliable means ...
- Being considerate means ...
- Being brave means ...
- Being strong means ...

Post-It Pride

Students are mixed up, pair up and are given a small pack of 'Post-It' sticky notes. Each person talks for 1 minute about something they have achieved – from passing an exam, to mending a bike, to learning an instrument or scoring a goal. As they talk, their partner identifies strengths that have gone into this achievement – such as determination, creativity, concentration and so on. They write each strength on a note and stick it on the person speaking. At the end of 2 minutes each person takes off the sticky notes, reads them and reflects on how they feel now about their achievement. They may thank their partner for noticing. This activity may need some discussion beforehand, placing strength cards in the centre of the Circle to remind students of possibilities and perhaps a demonstration. Let pupils know this is not a spelling test and the main focus should be on listening to identify strengths.

Internet Biography Searches

Ask pairs to identify someone well-known who they admire or find inspiring. They look that person up on the Internet and make a list of all the personal qualities they seem to possess and how these are demonstrated. By the time they have finished their search do they feel more positive about this person or less so? Why is that?

Personal Bests

A personal best can be in anything from a sporting endeavour to a level of reading to not losing your temper. If personal bests are not already part of class talk, students will need time to think about the concept before introducing this activity. Interview each other about:

- the personal best each is most pleased with
- the personal best they are going for this year.

Whole Circle Activities

Strength Cards

(These can be made or bought – see Appendix 3: Resources.)

Lay 'strength cards' out on the floor in the centre of the Circle and ask students to pick a quality or skill that they would like to have or develop. They tell the group or a partner why they have chosen this.

In pairs, each student is given a card and they tell each other how the qualities on this card apply to them. Each tells a story about how that strength was demonstrated.

Students are asked to choose a strength they admire in another person. Who is this person and how do they know they have this quality?

Guessing Good At

Turn to the person on your left or right and say: 'This is [name] and I am guessing she is good at [for example, reading, football, belly dancing, climbing trees].' The person then says: 'Yes, I am good at ... ', or 'No, I'm not good at ... but I am good at ...' [saying something that they are good at]. They then introduce the next person in the round and so on until everyone has had a turn.

Star of the Day

Each Circle session, one pupil becomes 'Star of the Day'. Everyone knows when their turn will come and no one is ever left out. This can be done around birthdays or simply a class list. Having this displayed is useful.

The 'Star of the Day' leaves the room. In the centre of the Circle is a large piece of paper. Students brainstorm everything positive about the person outside while the teacher writes this down. The 'Star' is invited back to hear what people have said about them. They are given the paper to take home or place in their Circle file.

Paddlepop Positives

YM

Each person writes their name on a paddlepop or ice-lolly stick and puts it in a pot. Everyone picks a name from the pot. They have a week to notice something positive about this person, something they do or say that they can tell the Circle about – the Circle might brainstorm the sorts of things to try to find.

Small Group Activities

Strength Statues

Give each small group a different strength card – this will depend on the age of the pupils. Ask the group to construct a statue – moving or still – that represents this strength. The rest of the Circle guess the strength depicted. They may need a list to choose from.

Strengths Stories

MS

Pupils plan and role-play a short scenario to illustrate a particular strength.

(Continued)

(Continued)

Extension Discussion

Think about the shadow side of strengths. For instance, if someone has the strength of confidence, they might be tempted to take risks, or if they are very caring, others might ask them to do too much.

Superpowers

Imagine each strength as a superpower. In small groups decide which superpowers would be helpful in the following situations:

- Having a row with a parent
- Being caught out in a lie
- Your pet dog (or cat) is very sick and probably won't make it
- Your family is going to move to another area away from all your friends
- Your older brother has broken something precious to you
- You are worried about the impact of climate change on your future
- You find out that a friend is bringing drugs into school

Extension Discussions

In what other situations might you need superpowers?
What strengths are particularly good in any situation?

Very Mild Superpowers!

David O'Doherty wrote a funny song in which he lists some of the strange things he is good at.

Just Google 'David O'Doherty and very mild superpowers' for a selection of video clips.

After students have watched David O'Doherty, ask them to list some very mild superpowers they can think of!

Dreams

Activities with a Partner

Aladdin's Lamp

(You may divide this activity up to discuss one wish at a time. You could also use stimulus materials, such as photos or symbols cards.)

(Continued)

(Continued)

Each student is given three wishes and partners tell each other what these are:

- Wish One: Something you would like to have
- Wish Two: Something you would like to do
- Wish Three: Something you would like to change about yourself

Extension Discussions

Give three reasons why each wish is important and then choose the most important.

If you could only have one of these wishes, which one would it be and why?

What would you wish for your family or your best friend?

For Older Students

How have your wishes changed since you were young?

Do you think they will change again?

There is a saying: *'Be careful what you wish for'*. What does this mean and why should you?

Dream Time   YMS

Give each student a piece of paper shaped like a cloud. On this they illustrate their dreams and hopes for the future in pictures and/or words. Pairs talk about their cloud dream to each other. Are their dreams similar or different?

Extension Discussions

What will you do to reach your dream?

Draw a ladder with the dream at the top and fill in the steps you might take to get there. What is important about the sequence of steps?

Do you think your dreams might change as you get older?

Life Map   MS

Each person has paper and pencil – they draw a road from one side to the other, then mark the most important events in their life, starting with being born. Each person in the pair talks about their life map to the other person.

Future Map   MS

This time the road begins with where the student is now and each person uses their imagination to plot a possible future for themselves. They may choose to draw several different roads, as there will be many possibilities. They share this with their partner and choose one goal to share with the Circle.

Values

Activities with a Partner

Pair shares and sentence completions

- One of the best things about being alive today is ...
- One thing we would like to do to make the world a better place is ...
- We both really look up to ... because ...

This is Me – and Me – and Me

Each person has a piece of paper divided into six. Sections have the following headings:

- Me at school
- Me as a son or daughter
- Me as a brother or sister (or grandchild)
- Me as a friend
- Me as part of a team
- Me by myself

Students draw and write down three things about themselves in each role. They then share with their partner and look for what is the same or different for each of them.

Extension Discussions

What other roles might we have in the future?

In which role do you like yourself most? Why is this?

Whole Circle Activities

Picture My Values

Spread out a large number of assorted photographs on the floor – these can be cut out from magazines or bought for the purpose – see Appendix 3. Each person chooses a photograph to illustrate one of the following:

- What is important to me at the moment?
- What are my hopes for the future?
- What would I most like to change about the world?

Each person explains why they have chosen this picture.

Valuing You   MS

Tape a piece of blank paper or card to the back of each pupil. Give everyone a thin coloured pen. The group mingle in the Circle and people write on the backs of their classmates (and teacher) anything about them they value. Students are encouraged to comment on those they know less well rather than special friends. When someone has written the fifth statement they take off the paper, fold it and give it to the person. No one may sit down or read their paper until everyone has five statements.

Reflection (this can take place as the closing activity)

Ask students to sit quietly and read what has been written about them. Ask them to think how this makes them feel about themselves and their classmates.

Time Capsule   MS

Each person in the Circle is given a shoebox or similar. They are to imagine that this will be their time capsule to be buried for 100 years. In this box they place anything that will tell the person who finds it all about them and the age in which they lived. This can include photos, drawings, favourite music or evidence of something that they like to do. Give students six weeks to do this. Then each person brings their time capsule to Circle sessions and small groups share the contents with each other.

Small Group Activities

Future World   S

Each small group has a large piece of paper. On this they draw and write what they hope for in the future world for their children.

- What would they like their children to learn?
- What do they hope their children will be able to experience?
- What would they like to be different for their children?
- What qualities do they hope for in their children?
- What would they like their children to feel about themselves/their family/the world in which they live?

Is there anything that each person can do now to make these things more likely in the future?

Embedding Circle Solutions as a Tool for Wellbeing

Are people aware of using strengths-based language to talk to and about students, families and colleagues?

Encourage students to identify strengths in other curricular areas such as in literature.

Download values from the Internet at the beginning of the school year. Put them up on the wall with a space underneath each one. Give each student 10 votes. Stickers are good! They vote on the values they want in their class this year. They can use all of these on one value or divide the ten up. In Circle sessions ask pupils to discuss the outcome and what this means for what will happen in the class. This gives students maximum agency for their classroom climate.

Class Wall of Strength

In Circle sessions students are given the opportunity to identify someone in the class who has shown a particular strength. This person is then given a brick-shaped card on which they write their name, the strength they have demonstrated and what they actually did. This 'brick' is placed on the wall so everyone can see how they are building their class wall of strength.

Strength Gotcha

The class focuses on one strength per week. This begins with a Circle session to help define what this means and then three 'gotcha' cards are handed out to all students. They give these cards to their classmates when they see them demonstrating that strength. No one can have more than three in the week. Everyone brings their cards to the next Circle and feeds back how they earned them and how they felt about showing this strength.

Perspective Glasses

The class teacher keeps a selection of cheap and cheerful spectacle frames in a box on the desk, the lenses having been removed. Each pair represents a strength, for example Good Listening, Good Sport, Leadership and so on. When a teacher notices that a student is demonstrating a particular strength they are allowed to wear those particular frames for the rest of the morning or afternoon. As they look through the glasses they identify other students who are showing the same strengths.

(Thanks to Sibila Gerden for this activity.)

5

Positive Communication Skills

> This chapter looks at how Circles can help to develop positive communication skills, and provides a wide range of activities to try out with students.

Good communication requires the following:

- the motivation to interact
- the opportunity to interact
- self-confidence
- clarity of meaning, expression and articulation
- congruence of verbal and non-verbal messages
- interest in others
- paying attention to what is being communicated
- understanding what is being communicated
- responding appropriately
- taking turns in speaking and listening.

Concentration span depends on age, development and learnt skills. The younger the child, the less complicated interactions and the more visual support they need. Children benefit from opportunities to interact even if they cannot yet use words. Many adults seem to have lost the art of conversation across a range of social situations. They may not show an interest in others and either speak *at* others or stay silent rather than enter a two-way dialogue. Students need to learn this vital art for whatever field they enter, from working in a shop to becoming a doctor. Positive communications oil the wheels of all relationships.

Circle activities in this chapter are focused on developing the following skills:

Focusing Skills

Before we listen we need to attend to the appropriate stimulus. We live in a world beset by distractions, and sometimes focusing on just one thing is hard to do. Activities here help children learn to focus.

Motivation and Confidence

Children are motivated to speak about things of real interest to them and where they feel safe. Those with little social confidence or poor language skills may happily join in with non-verbal games. Many teachers have said that children with 'selective mutism' have begun to speak in Circles.

Speaking Skills

People talk to one another for many reasons. These include:

- asking for something they need
- asking for information or clarification
- finding out about someone or something
- explanation
- demonstrating knowledge
- sharing experiences
- expressing feelings
- seeking support
- responding to others.

Conversation Skills

These include:

- showing interest
- taking turns
- responding to what others are saying
- having congruent body language.

Attention and Listening Skills

Today, more than ever, there are multiple demands for our attention. It is not surprising that many children and young people find it difficult to focus. The following activity helps reduce stimuli so pupils begin to learn to pay attention more specifically.

Passing Clouds   YMS

Begin the Circle with a minute of silence. During that time pupils are simply aware of thoughts passing or feelings they experience. All they have to do is notice them – perhaps imagine the thoughts in a passing cloud or identify where feelings are being experienced in their body. Nothing more. Signal when the minute is finished and thank the students. It may take practice but there is evidence this helps increase attention skills over time.

Listening is more than just hearing. Active listening requires focusing on another person and responding to what has been said. It is a powerful confirmation of the self to have someone really listen to you. Share pairs and interviews are opportunities both to practise listening and to be heard.

Sentence Completions

- Talking is easiest when …
- It is good to talk about …
- You know someone is listening when …
- When someone listens to what you say, you feel …
- When someone doesn't listen it makes you feel …
- It is difficult to talk when …
- It is difficult to listen to someone when …

Silent Statements

Stand up and change places if:

- you know someone who really listens to you
- you think you are a good listener
- you are good at talking
- sometimes you don't know when to stop talking!
- you have ever been at a loss for words
- you have sometimes said something you wish you hadn't
- you would like people to listen to you more

Activities with a Partner

Ask students to discuss this in pair shares and feed back with the following:

- A good person to talk to is …
- We like talking when …
- We like it when someone says …
- We need someone to listen to us when …

My Favourite Things

Each person interviews the other about their favourite things. Examples are:

- things to do on Sunday mornings
- people or places to visit
- a book, film or music.

Extension Discussion

What feelings are associated with some of these favourite things?

(Continued)

(Continued)

Variation

Children often find it easier and fun to talk together about things they don't like, for example:

- the nastiest thing you have ever eaten
- the most boring sport you can think of
- the worst TV program or film you have ever watched.

Active Listening Skills

First discuss how you can tell if someone is listening properly and what happens when they are not. Then each person chooses an experience they have enjoyed, such as a holiday, party or outing, and takes it in turns to tell the other. The listener begins by focusing on what is being said and responding by nodding, asking questions or commenting. At a given signal they stop listening, look away, interrupt or talk about themselves. Then the other person has a turn with the same sequence of listening and not listening.

Discussions

- What did it feel like to be listened to? What happened?
- What did it feel like not to be listened to? What happened?
- How can you tell that someone is really listening? What messages are given in the body, face, verbal responses? What are these?
- What do you agree are the two most important skills in a good listener?

Feed back to the Circle.

All Change

Pairs face each other and study what each is wearing for 1 minute. They then turn their backs to each other and change five things about their appearance: undo a button, put a ring on a different finger, comb their hair differently, fold a sleeve up, etc. When both say 'ready' they turn back to each other and see how many of these differences they can identify.

Encouragement

The pair makes a list of things to do or say to encourage someone to continue talking. They then try this out on each other.

Discussions

What did this feel like? Did it work?

Extension Activity

Make a list of things that teachers might say to encourage students.

Monologues and Dialogues

The same subject under different conditions highlights what it means to have a conversation and the skills involved.

Monologues

One of the pair has to speak for 30 seconds on a topic without repeating themselves or having too many pauses. The other person times them and notices if they are repeating themselves. Then they swap around. Subject ideas:

- favourite ice-cream
- learning to swim
- going to a park
- brothers and sisters
- homework

Conversations

Using the same category as before, the partners talk about the subject together for 1 minute, sharing experiences, ideas and views.

Discussion

- What is different about a monologue and a dialogue?
- Which is easier?
- Which is more enjoyable?
- What is another name for a dialogue?

Extension Activities

The pairs are given a subject, but this time one person asks questions and the other one makes statements. Then swap around.

Kim's Game

Put several small objects on to a tray. The number depends on the age of the children. This could include the following: a key, pencil, marble, whistle, toy car, coin, balloon, toothbrush, small ball, pair of scissors, elastic band, candle, eraser, bar of chocolate, button, earring, watch, box of matches, bus ticket, ribbon.

    Name all the items and then let the children look at the tray for 30 seconds. Cover the tray and ask pairs to write down as many as they can remember. Follow this up with a discussion about any strategies to help their memory (known as mnemonics). Did they group objects by use, colour, first letter or any other way?

Whole Circle Activities

Clapping Rhythms

The leader begins by clapping a simple rhythm and the children follow suit. The leader does this two or three times, then points at one of the children who does one clapping rhythm for the others to follow and then passes it along to someone else.

People Music

We can make music in many ways with our voices, hands and feet. The teacher, with students' help, chooses a song familiar to everyone and each person thinks for a moment about what they are going to use as their 'instrument'. They can hum, whistle, clap with their hands or on their knees, stomp with their feet, click their fingers or tongue or just sigh! No words. Everyone applauds at the end.

Birthday Lines

Everyone lines up according to their birthday, with January at the front – either with or without speaking – the latter is harder but more fun.

Variations

- Living nearest to/furthest from school
- Longest to shortest name
- Names in alphabetical order

(Do not use height as some children are sensitive to this.)

Social Bingo   MS

Each person is given the same 'bingo card' with nine squares and a pencil. Categories are written in the squares and pupils are asked to find someone that fits that category. For example: Someone who …

- has seen the same film as you – what film?
- has a birthday in the same month as you – which month?
- has a pet – what is the pet's name?
- can speak two languages – what are they?
- was born in a different country from you – which country?
- supports the same team as you (or none) – which team?
- likes the same food as you – what food?
- can ride a bike
- is left-handed
- has been to the dentist in the last month – did they have anything done?

Pupils sit back in the Circle when they have completed their card. As the teacher also participates, he or she will know how long the activity takes.

Heard You!

One person chooses to be blindfolded. They stand in the middle of the Circle. The other children pass round something that makes a noise such as a bell, a bunch of keys or a 'rain-stick'. When the person in the middle points accurately at the person holding the item, that person is then blindfolded (they can nominate someone else if they wish or have already had a turn). The game finishes when the object has been round the Circle at least once.

Going On Camp   YMS

Each person finishes this sentence with a phrase and an action. 'I am going to a camp and need to take ...' For example, if the word is 'boots' the student mimes pulling on boots, if it is 'toothbrush' then the action would be brushing teeth. On each person's turn they list everything that went before, also doing the actions, adding their object last. Other students help one another by doing the actions but not saying the word.

Variations

Change the first sentence:

- I'm going on holiday and in my suitcase I have packed a ...
- My friend is having a birthday party and I am going to take ...

Guess the Leader   YMS

One person leaves the room and someone in the Circle is nominated as 'the leader'. This person starts an action, such as tapping a foot, rubbing their head, clapping. Others follow suit. The person outside comes back and sees how quickly they can work out who is the leader as the actions change. Once they have been 'caught', the 'leader' becomes the one to guess. It is important for children not to look directly at the leader but to copy actions quickly.

Noises Off   YMS

Groups of students make a tape of about five sounds each. This is played to everyone and either pairs or small groups try and identify the sounds. Give each sound a time limit and then go on to the next. Ideas for sounds are:

- peeling a potato
- a lawnmower
- a toilet flushing
- eating an apple
- a kettle boiling
- someone swimming
- a zip fastener being closed
- hair being brushed
- pieces of paper being stapled together
- a car starting.

I See You

Everyone stands in a Circle looking down. The leader counts to three. On three, everyone looks up and looks directly to the person on their left, their right or straight ahead. If they make eye contact both shout 'Yes' and sit down. The game continues until everyone is sitting.

The Drawing Game   YMS

This game involves every form of communication except speech. It can be adapted to all age levels. Flexible and lateral thinking are encouraged.

The Circle is divided into groups of four or five, who gather in far corners of the room so others cannot hear them. Each group is given paper and pencils. The leader stands in the middle of the Circle with a list of 10 items or phrases suitable for the age and ability of the students. Someone from each group comes up to them and is secretly shown the first item. This person then communicates this to their group with the aid of drawing and mime. No words, either written or spoken, are allowed. When the group guesses correctly, someone goes and tells the answer quietly to the leader and is given the next item on the list. The group that finishes the list first wins.

Phrases may need to be communicated one part at a time, or words of one syllable at a time, so it is useful to indicate how many words or syllables are required by drawing lines on the paper. Older students might need to resort to charades-type clues such as touching their ears for 'sounds like' and miming messages such as 'shorter' or 'you are on the right track'. Students will enjoy being given the opportunity to devise their own lists and be leaders in this game. Examples of lists:

Y sunhat, shopping trolley, ice-cream, cat, shell, Christmas tree, birthday party, rainbow, aeroplane, whistle

M bus ticket, bar of chocolate, lipstick, lawnmower, storm, school assembly, bad dream, spider's web, glass of water, hot shower

MS horror film, winning a match, surfing the net, pantomime, exhausted, skiing holiday, breaking the speed limit, burst balloon, wet weekend, tantrum

S personal best, magic spell, alarm bells, peace and quiet, protest march, flat battery, big favour, frantic, lost in thought, storm in a teacup

One Word Categories   YMS

The Circle is given a category such as animals, colours, emotions, countries, etc. Everyone claps on their knees three times and then on the fourth stroke claps or snaps their fingers. The person whose turn it is adds a word in the category no one else has said before. If that word has already been said or the person cannot think of anything, that person is 'out' and sits in the middle of the Circle.

Single Word Stories   MS

Each person in the Circle says one word of a story so that the developing narrative makes sense, even if it stretches the imagination.

Extension Activity

Record the Circle stories and then write them up for display, perhaps with illustrations, so that the class can see what they have created.

Small Group Activities

At the Movies

Using sounds and gestures but not words, one person (or a pair) communicates an event to the rest of their group, who guess what is happening. Here are some examples:

- making tea and toast
- going to a see a funny film
- having a new puppy in the house
- learning to skateboard
- going to get your bike and finding it has a puncture

Extension Discussions

What helps you to understand what someone is trying to communicate in real life?

What do you pay attention to?

Sticky Labels Teamwork   MS

Divide the Circle into teams of about five or six. Teams are all given the same task. This could be one of the following but similar ideas are welcome:

- Design a new playground
- Plan a camping trip
- Plan a YouTube film to showcase something about your school

Before they begin their discussion, place a different sticky label on the forehead of each participant without them seeing what this is. These labels say one of the following:

- I'm the leader
- Ignore me
- Laugh at my ideas
- Agree with me
- Ask me questions
- Criticize me

Give students 5–10 minutes to discuss their task. At the end of that time each person takes off their label and talks to the others about their experiences of being treated accordingly. Give students time to reflect on this learning and in a subsequent Circle do the same activity again without labels.

Pupils talk about the difference it made this time around.

Embedding Circle Solutions as a Tool for Wellbeing

Good communication is critical in a classroom. Use the language of focus, attention, active listening and clarity with students. Positive communication needs to outweigh negative by about five to one. Questions are more effective in promoting thinking skills than statements.

Teachers often say a pupil is listening when they are looking at them but this is not necessarily true and can be culturally inappropriate. Someone can look at you and their minds be elsewhere, or they can be doodling and taking in every word. You know someone is listening when they respond to what you are saying – if they ask a question or add to the conversation.

Students who are distracted and unfocused cause teachers concern. There is evidence that these pupils have a higher than average resting heart rate, so calming activities may help reduce this. Encourage students to use mind maps to put their disjointed thoughts into some sort of order. Whenever they show control or increased focus, comment on how they are developing this strength.

Some students need to develop confidence to speak out. Using pair shares or small groups rather than asking individuals to come up with answers both reduces anxiety and promotes communication skills.

Some pupils are the ones to always want to give answers! Try giving them a set of 'contribution' cards at the beginning of the day and every time they answer they relinquish a card. When the cards are gone they have used up all their turns for the day – giving others more of a chance.

6

Emotional Awareness and Skills

> Activities in this chapter provide students with opportunities for talking about and reflecting on feelings in order to understand them more fully, develop a vocabulary to express more accurately how they feel, and begin to learn ways to feel better.

We are going to look at:

- knowing what emotions are for
- the ability to recognize and name emotions
- tuning into the physical sensations of emotions
- knowing what stimulates certain feelings, including interpretations of events
- increasing the vocabulary for safely expressing feelings
- knowing about emotional regulation – acknowledging and coping well with difficult feelings without letting them become overwhelming.

Talking about feelings can be challenging, so a safe and supportive Circle is crucial. Facilitators may choose to focus on positive feelings at first. In a class where you anticipate difficulties, start by keeping to the third person rather than expecting students to acknowledge their own emotions.

The lists below are feelings you might want to work with, depending on the age and stage of your class. As children develop more complex cognitive abilities, meanings change, so it is useful to revisit words. Some of the following are not theoretically emotions but are included here because children experience them as feelings. Many activities given in this chapter can be adapted to specific emotions.

Feelings in the early years:

- happy, friendly, loving, cuddly
- excited, surprised
- warm, cosy, comfortable, special, safe, loved
- unhappy, sad, hurt, sick, bad, funny, cold, hungry

- cross, grumpy, cranky, fed up, tired, sleepy
- bothered, scared, frightened

Additional feelings for 5- to 7-year-olds:

- pleased, cheerful, sparkly, lively, bouncy, successful
- interested, curious, able, strong
- lively, caring, cared for, concerned, fair, unfair
- muddled, confused, worried, unsure, silly
- shy, gentle, quiet, thoughtful
- disappointed, upset, tearful, sorry
- miserable, bad-tempered, angry

More feelings for 7- to 11-year-olds:

- delighted, enthusiastic, thrilled, fascinated, enjoying
- energetic, confident, keen, determined
- proud, thankful, relieved, amused, generous, affectionate, grateful, achieved
- included, important, trusted, valued, heard, cared for, understood, respected
- trusting, responsible, patient, brave, forgiving, sympathetic, understanding
- left out, ignored, rejected, let down, doubtful
- anxious, moody, irritable, frustrated
- flat, bored, down, exhausted, selfish
- shocked, horrified, disgusted, crazy, envious, furious, wild
- lonely, uncomfortable, embarrassed, stressed
- reluctant, indecisive, hesitant, helpless

Increasingly specific feelings for 11-year-olds onwards:

- satisfied, joyful, ecstatic, spirited
- serene, centred, appreciative
- acknowledged, supported, involved, appreciated
- independent, energized, motivated, anticipating
- courageous, resourceful, fearless
- in control, efficacious, absorbed
- empathic, altruistic, compassionate, apologetic
- apprehensive, ambivalent, fretful, awkward, distracted, disturbed, ashamed
- misunderstood, victimized, excluded, gutted, empty, outraged, appalled, chaotic, desperate, frantic, overwhelmed, out of control
- rejected, marginalized, defensive, envious, jealous, arrogant, complacent
- depressed, despairing, hopeless, isolated, impotent, impatient
- indifferent, apathetic, disengaged

Sentence Completions

- It is good to feel ...
- People feel [emotion] when ...
- Something that would make someone feel [emotion] would be ...
- It is easiest to learn something you when you feel ...

Silent Statements (with Reflections)

Stand up and change places if:

- you have ever felt proud of something you have done – relive that feeling now
- you are confident about being able to do one thing well – what helps you feel confident?
- something has excited you in the last year – what was this?
- something has made you sad in the last year – did you tell anyone how you felt?
- something has frustrated you in the last year – how long did this feeling last?
- you have felt scared and then felt brave – what happened to change the feeling?

Activities with a Partner

Pair Shares

- Find two things that make you both feel [emotion].
- Find two things that someone might do or say that help you to feel good about yourself.
- Find something that has happened to both of you that has made you feel [emotion].
- Find something that helps both of you feel better when you are [angry, upset, disappointed, frustrated].
- What helps you both bounce back when really difficult things have happened?

Feelings in Pictures

Students draw how they are feeling today and share this with their partner – can each guess what the other is feeling? How can they tell?

Extension Discussion

Does talking about feelings make any difference to the feelings?

Special People   YMS

Who makes us feel good? Our special people are not necessarily the same all the time. A footballer who scored a goal for our team last Saturday might be the person who makes us feel happiest all week. Students interview their partner about someone who made them feel good recently; what did they do or say? Is there anyone who does this a lot – do they have one special person, or are there several?

Extension Activities

Students draw their special person and write down all the things the person does and says that make them feel good about themselves.

Students draw themselves and write down all the things they can think of that they have done or said that have made someone else feel good.

Students interview each other about their pictures.

Mirrored Emotions

One person is the leader and expresses a given feeling, the other person mirrors this, copying as exactly as possible the body language and facial expressions of the other.

Extension Activities

The emotion is made larger or smaller by the mirror partner.

Opposites – the mirror tries to do the opposite of their partner.

Extension Discussions

When you are mirroring the emotion, do you feel differently according to what your body is doing? Does smiling make you feel happier, for example? How difficult is it to mirror the opposite emotion?

What do you feel towards someone when they have a smile on their face?

What do you feel towards someone when they look grumpy most of the time?

Dreams and Nightmares

Students interview their partner about their dreams. Do they remember what they dream about or do they fade quickly? Do they wake up with strong emotions in their body sometimes? What happens when they realize that these are based on a dream? Is it possible to have strong feelings sometimes that are generated by thoughts rather than by what is actually happening? What can be done about this?

Extension Discussions

What do filmmakers do to get us to feel strongly about a story?

How can people work up feelings of fear, anger, sadness and happiness in others?

Make a list of the strategies that are used. Can you think of instances where this has happened?

History and Culture

Begin with pair shares and sentence completions.

- Our families are proud of us when …
- Our families would be ashamed if we …

Small groups then discuss the following:

- How do we learn what behaviours are valued?
- Is this the same or different from one generation to another?
- Is this the same or different from one family and community to another?
- What does this tell us about where some of our feelings come from?

Whole Circle Activities

Happy, Sad, Excited, Scared

Go around the Circle giving students one of the words above. Ask them to change places when their emotion is called out and move according to the feeling with facial expressions to match. Add the words 'a little bit' or 'very' to emphasize different strengths of feelings.

The Smile

A rhyme for young children (use faces on cards for each expression):

A scowl and a smile

Met each other one day.

But somehow the scowl

Was not able to stay.

Facing the smile,

It just melted away.

Variations

Say the rhyme in pairs with one child doing the scowl and the other the smile.

Use faces on balloons and pop the 'scowl' at the end.

Faces

Have pictures that depict faces looking grumpy, sleepy, happy, sad and surprised.

Hold up one of the pictures and ask the children how this person feels. How can they tell?

Hold up one of the pictures and go round the circle with this sentence stem: 'I think this person feels grumpy/sleepy/happy/sad/surprised because ...'

The children change places if they feel the emotion being held up on the card:

- when they wake up in the morning
- when they go shopping
- when they go to a birthday party
- when they are asked to tidy their room.

Catch Me If You Can

Three volunteers close their eyes or are blindfolded while three marbles are passed quietly and separately around the circle. At a given signal, everyone puts their closed

(Continued)

(Continued)

fists on their knees. The people in the middle open their eyes and try to work out who has got the marbles by looking at people's faces. When they make a guess they tap that person's fist, who opens it up to reveal either the marble or an empty hand. Each person has three attempts at finding a marble. Those who still have undiscovered marbles at the end become one of the next finders.

Angry Alex

The students sit in a circle and one is given an apple to start the game. A piece of music is played by the teacher and whoever is holding the apple when the music stops becomes 'Angry Alex' and yells, 'Aaaarrrggghhh!!!!' (an angry sound). The Circle asks the student in chorus: 'What makes Alex angry today?' and the student gives an answer. The apple then continues around the circle until several students have had a turn. If the music stops at the same student more than once, they can hand the apple to another student to be Angry Alex.

Variations

Happy Henry, Frustrated Freddie, Stressed Samantha, Pleased Petunia.

Over the Top and Back Again

(Expressing emotions)

Half of the Circle stands up and approaches the centre of the Circle slowly. They begin by expressing an emotion in a mild way but build up to demonstrating this in an extreme way. Then they turn around and the emotional expression diminishes as they return to their seat. The other half then do the same.

Mad, Sad, Bad and Glad

All the emotion words at the beginning of this chapter can fall under one of these headings. Choose the section(s) that fit the class, put these words on cards and share them around the Circle in pairs. The students have to choose into which of the four categories their words will go. This provides an opportunity to talk about more complex aspects of feelings: when does excitement become mad instead of glad? When might they experience feelings that are sad and glad at the same time?

In the Manner of the Word

A pair of volunteers leaves the room while the rest of the Circle chooses an adverb such as happily, grumpily, frantically, thankfully, serenely, depending on the age of the students. The volunteers ask the whole group to mime actions 'in the manner of the

(Continued)

(Continued)

word'. If they cannot guess the word the first time, everyone is asked to carry out another mime. There are many possibilities for mimes, such as:

- eat spaghetti
- play cards
- wait for a bus
- play a guitar
- wash an elephant.

Perhaps put these ideas on cards. When one adverb has been guessed correctly, other volunteers leave the room and another adverb is chosen.

Now and Then

The Circle is given one the following words:

- humility
- modesty
- fidelity
- honour

They will debate the following motion: 'This Circle believes that [this value] is still important in today's world.'

The Circle divides into two groups: one will develop arguments to support the motion and the other will speak against it. Each group has 10 minutes to prepare their argument. The debate takes place with two speakers representing the group's view. The teacher asks at the end: 'Which people have been swayed by the arguments and have changed their mind from their original position?'

Bucket Fillers   YMS

We use up energy when we are active and replenish this when we rest and eat healthily. Everyone has an inner bucket of emotional resources. When it is full you feel happy, content and open to learning. When it is empty you feel miserable, angry or lethargic. Some people fill your bucket with generous, kind and thoughtful acts but others might do or say (or not do or say) things that dip into and empty your inner bucket.

A brightly coloured bucket is put in the middle of the room. Each pupil has a piece of paper and writes or draws something that raises their emotional resources, cheers them up when they are miserable or helps them keep their anger under control so it does not hurt anyone. They then screw up these bucket fillers and throw them into the bucket. Each person in turn takes out one a piece of paper and reads it out to the group.

Students could also make a list of Bucket Dippers – things that make you feel bad.

This is an excellent activity for embedding into everyday awareness.

Small Group Activities

Amygdala Moments

The amygdala is a small organ in the brain that is super-sensitive to any threat, perceived or real. It goes into action much faster than the neo-cortex, the thinking part of the brain, sending messages to the heart, lungs, arms and legs to prepare to respond. Overwhelmed by feeling we can react without thinking. The amygdala has good emotional memory and is vigilant – if we have already experienced major threats it gets triggered easily. Sometimes called an 'emotional hijack', this can get you into trouble.

In groups, brainstorm everything that gives someone an amygdala moment – what might make you very scared, or angry? Divide the list into three: threats that are real, possible or imaginary. Look at a threat from each list and discuss immediate options: fight, flight or freeze. When is your amygdala helpful? When do you need to wait for the thinking part of the brain to catch up? How does thinking help change how you feel and what you do?

The learning here is to only take immediate action when the danger is real – otherwise wait for your thinking brain to help you make better judgements.

Freeze Frame

One way to manage difficult emotions is to imagine the situation is happening in a film and that you are an observer. Role-play gives students an opportunity to practise this technique.

Each group of three pupils is asked to devise and act out a short scene that gives rise to one of these emotions: anger, fear, despair, panic. Scenarios could include:

- just missing a bus, which will make you late for something important
- being caught doing something that will get you into trouble
- being teased about your haircut
- getting your exam results today – you expect them to be really bad
- arranging to meet a friend who does not turn up.

At a point when the emotion is getting stronger, the leader calls out 'cut!' and everything stops. The group is asked to replay the scene so it has a different outcome.

Extension Discussion

What might you say to yourself in one of these situations that would help you manage it better?

I Feel It Here! YMS

(The embodiment of emotions)

Each group is given an outline of the human body and a feeling. The group talks about where that feeling is felt and write on the body what changes occur. Around the body

(Continued)

(Continued)

they list all possible stimuli to these sensations: what happens to increase the chance of the body responding in this way?

Extension Discussion

Is it what happens that causes the feelings or what we think is happening?

Could we put arrows from the external stimuli straight to the head and then from the head down to other parts of the body?

What influences how we think?

What Would You Notice?

Give each group a piece of paper. This represents a large room. At the moment there are people but no feelings in the room. Students begin by drawing in some people.

- What would you notice if happiness/helpfulness/respect/thoughtfulness/support/ friendship/acceptance were present in a room?
- How would people talk to each other? What might they be saying?
- What would their voices and the expressions on their faces be like?
- What might be happening?
- What would people be feeling? Would that feeling be catching?
- Would the room be somewhere people would want to be?
- The group writes and draws on the paper to illustrate its report back to the Circle.

Variations

How would you know if negative feelings such as anger, fear, intolerance, bad temper, or anxiety crept into a room?

How might you encourage them to leave? What is more likely to work?

Where Is the Feeling Now?

Each small group is given a set of words, each on a separate card but in no particular order. They are asked to arrange these from the mildest to the strongest:

- comfortable, content, pleased, happy, joyful, elated, ecstatic
- down in the dumps, sad, miserable, depressed, hopeless
- bothered, annoyed, irritated, cross, upset, angry, furious
- uncomfortable, worried, anxious, scared, frightened, terrified
- uneasy, concerned, embarrassed, guilty, ashamed
- interested, engaged, fascinated, absorbed, obsessed

When the group has done this it explains to the whole circle why it chose this order and the differences that are noticed as feelings get stronger.

(Continued)

(Continued)

Extension discussions

The group members decide when they are in control of the feeling and when the feeling might be in control.

What happens when feelings control you?

What things might stop a feeling getting the better of you?

Can you feel strongly without this being unsafe, e.g. extreme sports?

Was there a point where your over-the-top expression made you want to laugh at yourself?

The Mask

Each person is given a paper plate, string or ribbon and coloured pens. On one side of the plate they draw how they like to be seen by others. Inside they write or draw how they sometimes feel different from their 'public' persona. In small groups, each individual puts their mask up to their face and the others say what they see. They do not have to speak about their 'inner self' unless they choose to do so.

Extension Discussions

Is there a similarity between individuals in the ways they want to be seen?

What happens to the more difficult feelings inside the mask?

Catching Feelings

Divide the class into small groups of about four or five. They are given a simple task to do, such as plan an end-of-term party or draw a plan of the room. One person is secretly given a feeling and joins the group, demonstrating the feeling in the way they talk, the expressions on their face, their body language and their general demeanour. This can be either a positive emotion (enthusiasm, interest, calmness) or a negative one (boredom, misery, irritability). The others copy these 'symptoms'.

Extension Discussions

What difference does this make to the group?

What did group members feel?

Did it make a difference to completing the task?

How might you stop a negative emotion infecting the whole group?

Collages

Each group has a large piece of card along with collage material such as magazines, old cards, paint, feathers, stickers. They represent an emotion by making a collage of it. This can also be an individual activity with students presenting their collage to their group.

Moods and Music

YMS

Each small group is given a good-sized piece of modelling material. A two-minute piece of music is played while they listen. The group is then given 2 minutes to decide how they are going to mould the clay to express how the music makes them feel. The music is played again while they mould the clay. Each group shows their sculpture and explains why they made it that way.

Variation

Each small group is given a piece of paper and some coloured pens. (The same activity as above but this time, creating a picture.)

Alternative

Give individuals a piece of modelling material to mould, and each person explains to their group as above.

Extension Discussions

Does music change the way we feel?

Who uses music as a mood changer?

What else in our environment can change our mood?

Guess the Feeling

MS

The Circle is divided into groups of four or five. Each group is given a card with a different emotion. This will depend on the age and ability of the group. They are asked to decide what this emotion would be if it was:

- a colour
- an animal
- an item of food
- an item of clothing.

Each group says what their colour, animal, food and clothing are, and the rest of the Circle guess which emotion is being represented. (You could also think about this emotion as a car, sport, type of weather, shape, plant, sound, machine or place.)

Variation

Each group is given a word as above, but this time they make a still or moving statue representing the feeling and the rest of the Circle guess.

Embedding Circle Solutions as a Tool for Wellbeing

How might students learn more about emotions in other curriculum areas – biology, language and literature, arts, music, social studies, sport?

When there is a high level of emotion, ask students to tell you how they are feeling and then ask them to place this on a scale of 1 to 10 depending how strongly they feel it, with 10 being the strongest. Ask them what would help get it one point lower.

Have You Filled a Bucket Today?   YMS

Extend the Bucket Fillers activity from earlier in the chapter. Put a brightly coloured bucket in the classroom and when someone does something that helps fill someone's bucket the student writes it down and how it helped. This goes into the class bucket. For those who struggle with writing, others can help – which in itself is a bucket filler!

Introduce the idea of 'Play it Forward': When someone does or says something for you that helps fills your bucket you 'play it forward' and look for an opportunity to do this for someone else.

Students will begin to notice that when they begin to be Bucket Fillers for others this also helps fill their own bucket!

For further ideas, see www.bucketfillers101.com/free-resources.php

7

Promoting the Positive for Resilience

> This chapter looks at the evidence that resilience is developed by an optimistic outlook, predominantly positive feelings and being connected with others. There are suggested activities to promote these various aspects of resilience with students.

Although emotions cannot be positive all the time – that would be neither realistic nor appropriate – there is much we can do in educational settings to help students feel comfortable, safe and successful. We can also encourage them to take responsibility so their classmates feel the same way. Positive emotions enhance thinking skills and foster creativity and problem-solving. They also help undo the effects of negative emotion – people bounce back more quickly from adversity (Fredrickson, 2011). Having fun and laughing together promotes a sense of connection and raises levels of oxytocin – the 'feel good' neurotransmitter.

Sentence Completions

- This week I am looking forward to ...
- Today I am looking forward to ...
- This year I am looking forward to ...

Pair Shares

Pupils discuss the following and then feed back two things that they agree on:

- We are really pleased that ...
- It makes us laugh when ...
- The best thing about this school is ...

Table 7.1 What happened?

What happened?	How much was my fault? What could I have done instead?	How much was someone else's fault? What could they have done instead?	How much was down to chance and not anyone's fault?
You got sunburnt			
You got nearly all the words wrong on a spelling test			
You felt sick after a party			
You fell off your bike and broke your arm			

Activities with a Partner

Another factor that promotes resilience is taking appropriate responsibility. When bad things happen this is usually a combination of things you could have done differently, things someone else could have done differently and a big chunk of chance. If you blame yourself all the time this leads to depression; if you always blame others for your misfortune this eventually leads to feeling a helpless victim. Learning to get this balanced is useful.

Shared Blame

Share the situations in Table 7.1 with a partner and think about all the things that might have contributed. Have these things ever happened to you? How might you apportion blame in these scenarios? Give a score for each so that the total adds up to 10.

Optimistic Conversations

These are conversations that promote forward thinking and a focus on the good times.
   Remind students that these are conversations. This means that each person has a turn and their partner responds. Look for and comment on what you might share, rather than just wait for your turn!

- What made you laugh a lot in the last year?
- Where would you most like to travel to?
- The best feeling you had all week
- Your greatest adventure
- What would happen on your best birthday?
- Your dream for the future
- The biggest celebration you can remember
- The best game you ever played or watched

Extension Activity

Your partner draws your story as you are telling it.

Small Group Activities

Perspectives

Copy this picture and show it to small groups. Ask them: what do you see? Allow them to answer and then ask: Can you see both pictures – a young lady and an old woman? Tell them there is no right or wrong way to see this picture.
   Ask pupils to discuss whether or not it is possible to see life in different ways.
   Some people say that it is not what happens to you that matters, but how you see it. Do you agree?

(Continued)

(Continued)

Figure 7.1 Perspectives

Photocopiable:
Circle Solutions for Student Wellbeing © Sue Roffey, 2014 (SAGE)

What different ways could you think about and respond to the following situations: can you think of anything good that might come out of them?

- Losing a match
- Not getting something you wanted
- Not being able to go on holiday because someone in the family is ill

Headlines

Ask students to think about a time they made a mistake or something didn't go right. They begin by taking turns to talk about this event under the headline 'Disaster'. Then they talk about the same event but this time the heading is 'Success'. In this story they talk about anything positive that came out of this challenging situation.

The War for Wellbeing

This activity introduces imaginary characters that help determine whether someone becomes an optimistic person who looks for solutions or someone who is likely to become miserable and helpless, buried in their problems and not seeing a way out. Everyone has difficulties to deal with, though some are tougher than others. The voices in our head can give us positive or negative messages. Here they are personalized as Grimy Goblins or Good Graces.

(Continued)

(Continued)

The Negative Voices are the **Grimy Goblins**. These can attack your wellbeing:

- **The Sprite of Bad Stories** (SOBS) wants you to see the bad in everyone and the bad in everything. She loves to make the most of when things go wrong and is full of blame, which makes you feel miserable and not good at anything.
- **The If-Only Elf** wags a finger and says 'if only you had done that, this wouldn't have happened'. He makes you feel guilty and wrong about everything.
- **The Worry Wart** – If you are not careful she will turn into a Panic Monster. She tells you everything that might go wrong (it usually doesn't) and makes you feel anxious and scared to try new things or even do your best with familiar ones.
- **The Doom Merchant** uses the words Always and Never, such as 'It is *always* raining' and 'We *never* have any fun'. This can make you feel angry or resentful.
- **The Misery Maker** infects everyone with his scowls, frowns, groans, sighs and whinges. We are all sad about something from time to time but the Misery Maker is more than just sad, he can't see the positive in anything. No one likes to be in his company for long because he drags people down and makes them feel empty and helpless. You hear him say 'Yes, but …' a lot.

The **Good Graces** are the Positive Voices that help keep all the Grimy Goblins in their place, stop them taking over your thoughts and help protect your wellbeing. They are:

- **Common Sense** who asks good questions about what can help you out of a tricky situation. She is very matter of fact and likes to check on the evidence. 'How do you know that?', she will ask. 'Are you jumping to conclusions or letting your imagination run away with you?' She also reminds you of all the strengths you can put to good use. She can help you feel hopeful and strong.
- **Beautiful Blessings** reminds us of everything there is to be thankful for – from little everyday things to more significant life blessings. Beautiful Blessings helps you feel contented and grateful.
- **Organization Owl** is serious minded and helps keep thoughts in order so they don't run all over the place tripping themselves up. He will say: 'What do you need to do next? What will help? What can you look forward to next week?' He helps you feel more in control of things.
- **The Mindfulness Magician** stops us worrying too much about what happened in the past and what might happen in the future. He puts a bubble around the moment you are in and helps you savour the good things. This can help you feel calm and peaceful.
- **The Positive Thinking Pixie** is a great problem solver and gives you ideas of things you might do in a tricky situation. She is able to find something positive in anything or anyone, including learning from your mistakes, finding opportunities to use your strengths and seeing the best in people. She often sees the funny side of things. She helps you feel optimistic and energized.

There are numerous activities that can engage students in using these characters. Some are given here but imaginative teachers will be able to think of many more. Older students can be asked to write their own stories or visualization, perhaps for use with younger pupils.

Paired or Small Group Discussions and Activities

Sometimes it feels right to be sad or upset. When might that be?

Difficult times happen to everyone – they are normal. Difficult times might open the door to the Grimy Goblins. How can we keep them out and stop them taking over?

(Continued)

(Continued)

Think about each Grimy Goblin as a voice in your head. What sorts of things would they each say? Make a list.

Vote for the Grimy Goblin you like the least. Is it:

- The Sprite of Bad Stories who whispers things that make you feel stupid or unloved?
- The Panic Monster who tells you that you can't do things and makes all challenges look very scary?
- The If-Only Elf who pretends to help but never with ideas that really work?
- The Misery Maker who blows difficulties out of proportion so your bad thoughts and feelings can't let any good thoughts and feelings in?
- The Doom Merchant who infects you with hopelessness which can make you feel angry?

Put the Grimy Goblins in order of how much they might impact on your life.

Do you know anyone who has given a home to a Misery Maker? What do you feel when you are near them? What might help this person kick the Misery Maker out?

Think about each Good Grace as a voice in your head. What sort of things would they each say? Make a list.

Vote for your favourite Good Grace.

Blessings can be a real friend. What do you have in your life that you are thankful for? In your pair or group make a list of five big blessings that you all agree on and each person thinks of one little blessing that has happened for them this week.

How might the Mindfulness Magician help someone?

What experiences would you want in your magic mindfulness moments? Which would you want to savour the most? What would you feel when you are there, not worrying about the past or the future?

It what situations would you need the Positive Thinking Pixie?

Paired or Small Group Creative Activities

Small groups draw one of the characters or make a collage. One or two people can draw while others give ideas about what they might look like, wear, hold in their hand, say and have around them.

One group takes on the roles of the five Grimy Goblins and one group takes on the roles of the five Good Graces. One person takes on the role of the 'Thinker'. The Goblins and Graces battle it out to win over the Thinker. Scenarios could include any of the following:

- Falling out with a friend
- Losing a match
- Failing a test
- Spreading a nasty rumour
- The death of a pet
- Telling a lie about not doing your homework
- Planning a party
- A family change

Each Goblin and Grace says one thing each: the groups can decide beforehand what these are going to be. Students then role-play the whole 'battle' for the Circle. First the Thinker tells everyone what is on his or her mind then the Goblins and Graces try to influence what the Thinker feels and does. The Thinker gives feedback on what happened, what helped and what didn't.

Who Says What?   YMS

In pairs decide who of the Grimy Goblins or Good Graces would say the following in your head:

- It does nothing but rain.
- The rain is horrible.
- I just love the sound of the rain on the roof – it feels cosy being inside.
- This rain will be great for the garden.
- Check you have everything you need for the morning.
- If only you hadn't said that.
- You really upset her, she won't want to be your friend now.
- You don't know that – perhaps just saying sorry will help, you won't know until you try.
- I wouldn't go and apologize, it will only make things worse.
- Next time I won't be so quick to jump in.

Success Stories   S

(You may want to separate these discussions rather than attempt all at once.)
   Find one thing that has made each of you feel successful. What happened?
   What do advertisements tell us about being successful? Why do they do this? Should we believe them?
   Is someone always successful if they have fame or fortune?
   Are success and happiness always the same thing?

Thanks in a Hat   YMS

This is in two parts. The first is a sentence completion in the round to raise awareness of possibilities: 'I could say thank you for …'. Suggest that people are specific: not just for 'helping me', but 'helping me with …'; not just 'being a friend', but 'being a friend by …'.
   Each person puts their name on a piece of paper and puts it into a container. The container is shaken up and then everyone takes a name out. Each person reads out the name and says: 'I would like to thank … for …'.

This Class Says Thank You   YMS

The Circle brainstorms all the people who do things for the class in any way. This could include the caretaker, administrative staff, cleaners and so on. Each small group takes one of these people, discusses what this person does, how they help the class and the difference that they make. The group then makes a card that expresses the thanks of the class. Also, the group takes responsibility for delivering it to that person.

Circle Activities for Laughter and Positive Emotions

Laughter promotes oxytocin, the 'feel good' hormone, and when this is shared it increases a sense of belonging.

Whole Circle Activities

Mrs Mumbleby

This simple game was shared by a wonderful group of school counsellors in Queensland. I have since used it with children, teenagers, adults, and once with a conference of over 200 people sitting around tables! As well as producing uncontrollable mirth, it brings everyone to the same level.

The leader turns to the person on their right and says: 'Excuse me, have you seen Mrs Mumbleby?' The reply is: 'No, I haven't but I'll ask my neighbour.' They then turn to the person on their right and repeat the question. This goes around the Circle until everyone has had a turn. Everything is said, however, with your lips turned inward as if you have no teeth.

The Laughter Chain

Half of the class lie in the centre space with their heads on each others tummies forming a circle. One person starts by laughing. As you laugh your tummy wobbles. When the person feels the wobble they also start laughing and so on, until the laughter chain reaches around the circle. Ask the rest of the class if they could see the laughter chain moving. Now the other half of the class does the same thing. This time, they have to try not to laugh until they feel the tummy-wobble of the person before them.

Extension Discussions

Does it make you feel good inside when you can't help laughing?

Was it difficult to stop laughing? What made it even more difficult to keep a straight face?

Does it make you feel more positively towards everyone else?

Is it a different feeling when you are laughing at someone in a hurtful way or with someone in shared fun?

Small Group Activities

Punch lines   YM

Find the right punch line to these jokes. In groups students work out which joke goes with which punch line.

(Continued)

(Continued)

Table 7.2   Punch lines

1	What medicine would you give to an ill ant?	The Lizard of Oz	A
2	What do you call a fish with no eyes?	Lots of blood tests	B
3	What would you get if you crossed a vampire with a teacher?	Because it was framed	C
4	When a knight in armour was killed in battle what sign did they put on his grave?	Because 7 8 9	D
5	Doctor, how do I stop my nose from running?	Fsh	E
6	Why did the picture go to jail?	Your legs	F
7	What weighs more: a ton of feathers or a ton of bricks?	Antibiotics	G
8	What powerful reptile is found in the Sydney Opera House?	Rust in peace!	H
9	Why is 6 afraid of 7?	They are both the same	I
10	What has a bottom at the top?	Stick your foot out and trip it up	J

Photocopiable:
Circle Solutions for Student Wellbeing © Sue Roffey, 2014 (SAGE)

The following week ask the group to make up three more jokes together. They may need to research this.

Extension Discussions

What makes a good joke?

When is a joke not a joke?

Embedding Circle Solutions as a Tool for Wellbeing

Make a Book of Blessings for the class.

Encourage students to have a Positive Feedback (PFB) File, where they keep all of the positive comments they have been given about themselves and their achievements – the more specific the better. When a student is having a particularly bad time, encourage them to read their PFBs to remind them that this is only temporary, they have many strengths, good things have happened to them before and will do again. Students need to take their PFB File all the way through school. It is important that this is not seen as competitive and everyone, especially the more vulnerable students, has plenty of material to draw on.

Use the imaginary characters in this chapter to help students identify their mindsets and promote more positive ones.

When there are incidents ask pupils to identify how much out of 10 was their fault, how much someone else's and how much just bad luck. Give them some time to work this out. This will help them to accept what was down to them and take appropriate responsibility.

When someone says 'It was only a joke' ask them if everyone was laughing. Help students to understand the difference between laughing *with* and laughing *at*.

8

Shared Humanity: Connection, Belonging and Empathy

> **This chapter promotes inclusive belonging to foster both resilience and a supportive class community. Activities are aimed at encouraging pupils to know one another well, discover what they have in common, break down stereotypes and weaken cliques. We honour the uniqueness of individuals and diversity in the class but also seek and celebrate our shared humanity. This is the opposite of exclusive belonging that can promote intolerance and dehumanize others. Several activities in this chapter go beyond the immediate class to wider social issues to address prejudice and promote empathy.**

People are often marginalised or even bullied because they are different in some way. This chapter helps pupils understand the importance of valuing and including others.

Sentence Completions

- The best thing about this school is …
- This class is great when …
- Someone would feel welcome in this class when …
- You would look forward to coming to school if …

Pair Shares and Sentence Completions

- We feel valued when …
- When someone smiles at us we feel …
- When someone asks us to join in we feel …
- When we are having a hard time it helps when …
- We all need help when …
- We feel supported when …
- The best day we had in this class was when …

Silent Statements

Stand up and change places if:

- you have ever asked someone to join a game you are playing
- you have ever offered help to someone who is stuck on a work problem

- you have been able to ask for help
- you have been willing to lend something to a classmate
- you have returned borrowed things
- you have ever stuck up for someone who was being bullied.

Activities with a Partner

Ask pairs to find two things they share and are happy to say to the Circle. Examples include:

- activities you both like doing at school
- things you both like doing at home
- what you both like about this school
- what you both like about this class
- words and/or actions that would make someone feel they belong here
- positive things you have said at home about this class
- something you could both do that would make this class better for everyone.

Whole Circle Activities

Picture Me

Everyone has a piece of paper and pencil. In pairs, pupils interview each other, finding out what they are interested in. They sketch these on the paper – the only writing is the person's name. After 3 minutes the pieces of paper are sent five places around the Circle. Each student introduces the person whose name is on their paper and talks about their interests. There is a brief right of reply to correct any inaccuracies.

Jump To It!

Everyone stands up and holds hands. The facilitator asks students to jump forwards or backwards if the following applies to them. Statements in List A will apply to some and not others – List B applies to everyone. Students can be asked to call out 'Me' or 'Everyone' as they jump.

Table 8.1   Lists A and B

List A	List B
You have brown eyes	You need to learn new things
You have been to more than one school	You need someone to look after you
You like reading	You need clean water to drink
You watched TV last night	You need to feel safe
You are good at drawing	You need to have a home of your own
You have given someone a present	You need to stay healthy

Photocopiable:
Circle Solutions for Student Wellbeing © Sue Roffey, 2014 (SAGE)

The 100 Person Village

Google '100 person village' and you will get a selection of videos that show proportions of people who would be a certain race or religion, have a certain level of income, education, health care, food, access to clean water and so on, if the world were a village of just 100 people. (You will need to check which is most appropriate for your class and ensure that any comments associated with the video clips are screened.)

The following discussions take place in small groups who then report to the Circle:

- What did the film make you feel about your own situation?
- What do you think is the most powerful of these statements?
- What is open to change and what is not?
- If you could change one thing what would it be and why?
- Do those with everything have a responsibility to help those with nothing?

Fox and Rabbit

Everyone sits on the floor with their legs stretched out in front towards the centre of the Circle. Two soft toys are placed on ankles at opposite sides of the Circle. At a given signal the group attempts to move these around the Circle without touching them with their hands, trying to get one animal catch (or escape from) the other before it gets back to where it started. Give students a practice run first. This can get quite rowdy!

Class Web

Everyone stands up. The leader has a ball of string, holds one end tightly and throws the ball to someone else saying their name. This person holds onto the string, the connection is tightened and they throw the string ball to someone else. This continues until everyone is included and the web has been made. The facilitator comments on the importance of everyone in the group being part of the web and if one person drops out the whole web breaks.

Circle Knot

This activity demonstrates that whole groups of people can get themselves into knotty situations and that it is up to everyone to work out a solution.

Everyone stands up, and joins right hands. Then they join left hands with a different person. They all then move anywhere they want so long as they do not let go. After 20 seconds the group will be in a knot and now have to try to untangle themselves, again without letting go of one another's hands. If this works, the Circle will reform with some people facing in and some facing out.

Flour Cake

Put a gold chocolate coin or something similar in the centre of a bowl and fill the bowl with flour, packing it down firmly. Turn the bowl upside down onto a plate to form a 'cake'. This is placed in the centre of the Circle. Everyone has a turn to take a teaspoon of flour from the cake and put it in an empty bowl. The aim is to get around the group at least once before the flour cake collapses. The person holding the teaspoon when this happens has to retrieve the coin with their teeth, getting their face covered with flour!

Purple World

This is taken from an activity suggested by the UK's Qualifications and Curriculum Authority to address racism. To build on this see: http://bit.ly/10qPPTh

The teacher tells a story about a world where everything is purple – clothes, food, cars, houses and schools. The only food is purple soup, which everyone eats at the same time. Students talk in pairs about what it would be like if everything was the same – would they like it or not? This activity is followed by sentence completions:

- If everything was the same ...
- Being different is good because ...

Something About You

Pupils stand in two concentric circles facing each other. Pairs have 30 seconds to find one thing they have in common and one thing that is different. After 30 seconds the facilitator calls 'time'. The outer circle takes a step to the right and the inner circle goes in the opposite direction so everyone has a new partner. They do the same thing again. Repeat this three or four times.

Here Be Monsters

An adventurer needs to overcome obstacles and challenges to reach the treasure. Success depends on support from the whole Circle.

One student volunteers to be the adventurer who will cross the dangerous land of monsters to reach the pot of treasure. He or she is blindfolded but have a support team to show them the way and keep them safe.

On an empty chair is placed a bag of treasure. This could be stickers, gold chocolate coins or other small items. There must be enough for everyone. Several 'monsters' and other dangers are placed across the middle space. Plastic dinosaurs, sharks, toy lions, etc, can be used, as well as boxes for mountains and pieces of paper for lakes. Pupils might like to make their own 'monsters' and other obstacles. The adventurer begins from the opposite side of the Circle and everyone helps negotiate the dangers to collect the treasure. They give instructions of where and how far to move and when to stop.

(Continued)

(Continued)

There are several ways to do this. Either each pupil takes a turn to give an instruction, or the class can shout out when the adventurer is in danger, tell them to stop and which way to go. Perhaps start the game by asking the Circle what the best strategy would be. They might use signs, perhaps a whistle for stop and clapping for going forward.

The 'treasure' is shared with the class in a gesture of solidarity and thanks.

Extension Discussions

What sorts of difficulties or monsters might someone in this class face?

How might people in the class support someone who is having a challenging time?

Rescue!

Students have to work together to get everyone to safety. This activity is worth doing several times consecutively to improve outcomes.

Three students are in the original rescue team. Everyone else is unconscious in the burning building (lying motionless in the middle of the Circle). No one can help to rescue anyone else until they have been rescued themselves and taken to a safe place outside (a point outside the circle). Once they have been rescued, they join the rescue team. The building will blow up in 4 minutes. Can everyone get to safety before it does? Aim for class bests and talk about what worked well and how to do it better next time. You may want to discuss fire safety as a conclusion to this activity.

Small Group Activities

What Do We Know?

This game has valuable outcomes in understanding how easy it is to jump to conclusions about people before you know more about them.

Each small group is given a picture of an object, such as lunch-box or hat, alongside the gender and age of the owner (see the examples below). The group is asked to talk about what this person might be like. They agree three statements based on the information given. They are then given an envelope containing three to five additional pieces of information. They take these out one at a time. Some are positive and some negative. You will need to devise statements appropriate for students in your class. They might include things like:

- This person is a carer for a parent who has multiple sclerosis.
- This person's parents are splitting up.
- This person hid while their father was taken away – they haven't seen him since.
- This person can speak three languages.
- This person can play the guitar.
- This person lives on a farm and gets up at 5am to help with the animals.

As each statement is read out they revise their understanding of what the person might be like and any significance the object might have. The discussion following this activity asks the following questions:

(Continued)

(Continued)

- How close was your original thinking to your final thinking – how much did your view change?
- Did you feel differently about the person as you knew more about them?
- What does this tell you about jumping to conclusions?
- Can you relate this to situations in real life?
- Do we sometimes make judgments on incomplete information?
- Has someone judged you before they knew the circumstances?
- What have we learnt from this game?

These books belong to a boy aged 12	**These trainers belong to a girl aged 16**

Statements in envelope:	Statements in envelope:
He is hearing impaired. He is the oldest child in a large family. His grandparents live at home. He loves football. He is very frightened of dogs.	She works on Saturdays in a petrol station. She hopes to become a doctor. Her parents speak very little English. She is a black African. She is in training for running a marathon.
These glasses belong to a girl aged 8	**This doll belongs to a girl aged 5**

Statements in envelope:	Statements in envelope:
She lives in a mobile home with her mum. She has a beautiful singing voice. She lost her younger brother in an accident two years ago. She does most of the cooking at home. She is being bullied at school and on social media.	She is popular with teachers because she always wants to please. She is the youngest of three children, all have spent time in care, though she is now living back at home. Her father is in prison for violence. She loves stories. She is allergic to dairy foods.

Figure 8.1   Examples for use in 'What do we know?'

Photocopiable:
Circle Solutions for Student Wellbeing © Sue Roffey, 2014 (SAGE)

Give Us a Clue

This activity is intended to develop empathy with those who cannot read well or have a struggle with understanding language.

Copy the following text and clues and give a copy to everyone in the Circle. Ask everyone to try to work it out by themselves for the first 2 minutes, then in a pair for 5 more minutes, then in groups of four. Start by looking for the slightly larger gaps between words.

[coded sentence in symbols]

Clues are:

- **❶❀❀** is 'the'.

- **⑩❶❶ɑℛ❀❺❶⑩** is 'students'.

- **✍⑥⑥ɑ** is 'good'.

- **ɑ** is, 'a', **⑤** is 'n' and **ɛ** is 'c'.

Figure 8.2   Coded sentence

Photocopiable:
Circle Solutions for Student Wellbeing © Sue Roffey, 2014 (SAGE)

When the time is up, show the answer. It is a quote by William Glasser:

> Running a school where the students all succeed, even if some students have to help others to make the grade, is good preparation for democracy.

Students then discuss in small groups:

- What helped you be more successful, doing this on your own or with others?
- What did you feel when trying to work this out?
- How would you feel if you had this difficulty all day, every day?
- What does the quote mean? Do you agree with it?

Extension Discussions

In what other situations is it a struggle to understand communication?
Has anyone got a story that illustrates this?

Extension Activity

Ask groups of students to prepare a similar quote in code.

Our Class

Small groups are given card or canvas in the shape of a flag or shield and some collage materials. Groups talk about what would represent their class. They then construct a flag or shield that reflects their discussion. Each group shares their collage with the Circle.

This Class Cares

Each discussion takes place in a separate Circle and decisions are followed through.

- What can we do to welcome someone new to this class?
- What can we do to help someone new to fit into this class?
- What would we want a new person to think about this class?
- What can we do to welcome someone back when they have been away for a long time?
- What can we do to learn about one another and one another's families?
- What might help someone who is always left out?
- What might help someone who struggles to understand what to do?

Absent But Not Forgotten

Sometimes an individual is absent from the class for a length of time because of illness, bereavement or even suspension. Showing that student that they are still part of the class not only makes them feel supported but also promotes an ethos that everyone matters. Groups are given card, stickers and felt pens. They discuss what is going to go on the card for the student to show them that their classmates are thinking of them. What words will go on it, and who will write them? What illustrations will there be? The teacher takes responsibility for sending the cards to the student concerned.

Understanding Impairment and Difficulties

The following activities give students an understanding of what it is like to have a visual or hearing impairment, physical or social difficulties.

Visual Impairment

The Jelly Wobble

Four students volunteer to be blindfolded. Pairs sit opposite each other in the middle of the Circle and are covered with protective clothing. Each person is given a bowl of jelly and a spoon. The aim of the game is for each person to feed the jelly to their partner until the bowl is empty. The first pair to do so wins. If noise isn't a problem, the rest of the Circle can call out helpful directions. This game is good fun!

In the Dark

Divide pupils into groups of three and place several obstacles in the centre of the Circle. One student volunteers to be blindfolded and the others slowly lead this pupil around the Circle, not tripping over anything or bumping into other groups. Each student in the trio can have a turn of being blindfolded and taken around the Circle.

In your groups, discuss the following:

- What did it feel like not to be able to see where you were going?
- How did you feel about the two people who were guiding you?
- What enables you to trust somebody?
- What can you imagine are the difficulties for someone who can't see properly?
- What sort of things might they need in order to live as near normal a life as possible?
- What does it feel like to be responsible for someone's safety?
- What does it mean to be trustworthy and is it a good feeling?
- Can you always tell if someone can't see properly?

Hearing Impairment

Seeing Is Hearing

All students cover their mouths with a scarf and engage in conversation with one or more other pupils about something that happened at school in the last couple of days. How easy is it to hear someone when their face cannot be seen properly?

Then everyone either puts head-phones on or uses ear-plugs. How easy is it now to make out what someone is saying? The teacher plays some loud music or a tape of playground noise. Does this make a difference to the ability to understand?

Whole Group Discussion

What does this tell you about what people with a hearing impairment need?

Physical Difficulties

The Drawing Challenge

Each person has a piece of blank paper and a pencil. They draw a picture of someone else in the Circle and write this person's name using their non-dominant hand.

Small group discussions

What feelings did you experience doing this activity?

Has anyone broken their arm or wrist so they couldn't use it for a while?

What other things would be difficult to do when you can't use one arm? Make a list.

What sort of help would someone need if they had this sort of difficulty?

(Continued)

(Continued)

Do you know anyone who has a physical disability? What adaptations do they have to make in their lives?

Imagine being in a wheelchair. Check out how many slopes and steps there are from your house to school or in your local shopping centre.

Variation

Draw or paint a picture holding a pencil or brush in your toes or mouth.

Social Impairment

The Sixth Sense

(For more ideas see Carol Gray's book of the same name.)

Ask students to talk in pairs about how information gets into our brains. The aim is for them to identify the five senses – sight, hearing, touch, taste and smell. People who have impairment in one or more of these senses need help, as we have seen. There is a sixth sense, sometimes called the social sense. This is the ability to understand someone else's perspective – to be able to imagine what is in their minds and hearts. Give pairs this picture of a cat stuck in a tree with someone attempting a rescue and ask students to make a list of what the rescuer might be thinking and feeling. In this activity you are using your sixth sense.

Figure 8.3   Cat rescue

Photocopiable:
Circle Solutions for Student Wellbeing © Sue Roffey, 2014 (SAGE)

(Continued)

(Continued)

Some people find it difficult to understand something from someone else's point of view. Sometimes (but not always) this is because students in this position have Asperger's Syndrome or might be on the Autistic Spectrum.

Double pairs up to make a group of four. Ask them to think about how social impairment might affect someone. If they are not able to do this easily give them the following list to help.

Would someone with social impairment:

- always know when it is their turn?
- be able to talk about what happened to them?
- find it easy to have a conversation about what happened to other people?
- understand why people might do things?
- sometimes be frightened?
- be able to easily follow the rules of a game?
- make friends easily?

Now ask them to discuss what sort of help someone like this might need.

Extension Activity

Look up some famous people, such as Bill Gates, who have had social impairment.

Visiting Strange Lands

Divide the Circle into two groups. One group is the Maxis and the other the Minis.

Each group is told only about their own cultural expectations, what people do in *their* country. Groups spend 5 minutes with their 'own people' practising what to do. Then they start to 'visit' each other. This 'cultural exchange' is to foster good international relations. Everyone needs a 5-minute visit.

The Maxis:

- greet each other by putting out their tongue and wagging their hand behind their head
- are very interested in all water sports and often want to talk about this
- think that people with brown eyes are the most important
- avoid touching one another in public in any way
- have a great sense of humour.

The Minis:

- greet each other by grabbing the other person's arm with both hands and looking deep into their eyes
- are very interested in all ball games and often want to talk about this
- think that people who are short or wear glasses are especially wise
- avoid laughing in public
- breathe very deeply when they are upset about anything.

Discussions

Did you feel a sense of belonging (affinity) with your original group?

Did you feel confused when you went for a visit?

(Continued)

(Continued)

How did you learn what to do?

Did you mind trying to be different from your first group so you could 'fit in'?

List what you have learned from this activity.

Extension Discussions

What experiences have some people had before they arrive in a new country?

What difference will this make to how they feel about being there?

What do you think people miss about their old country?

What might help them to settle in?

Worm Game

Give out a set of cards, half of which have a picture of an apple and half have a picture of a worm. Just one has a picture of a fisherman. One child begins the game as Jimmy or Jemima worm and goes up to someone in the Circle and says: *'I am Jimmy (or Jemima) worm – are you my brother/sister?'* The child either says: *'Yes, I am',* and attaches themselves in front of the worm, or says: *'No, I am an apple, you can eat me to grow longer and stronger',* and joins the back of the line. The child at the front then approaches someone else in the Circle with the same question. When they get to the pupil who has the fisherman card s/he says *'Hello, worm. Come fishing with me'* and tries to catch one of the 'worms' before they are either 'safe' back on their chairs or are 'protected' by an apple who puts their arms around a worm's shoulders.

Embedding Circle Solutions as a Tool for Wellbeing

Students who are seen as different in some way are often the target of bullying. Inclusive belonging is therefore critical. All pupils need to feel they belong, that they are safe and that they can participate and contribute. This has implications for how lessons are structured and the language used to promote individual value.

Where there is 'exclusive' belonging people can be dehumanized because they are not seen as 'one of us'. Discussions with middle primary and senior students need to reflect on what happens beyond the school gates.

Activities can be followed up by exploring personal stories, investigating linked websites and using literature to promote further understanding (see Appendix 3: Resources).

9

Friendship, Cooperation and Ethics

> This chapter contains activities to reflect on what it means to be friendly, the qualities that we seek in friends, and the skills involved in becoming and being a good friend. We also address group behaviour – group collaboration and how people might maximize everyone's wellbeing. Responsible and ethical behaviour includes being aware of how decisions affect others and taking account of this.

Friendliness can be defined as 'appropriate' social behaviour and positive interactions with others – often referred to as social skills. This is a pre-requisite to the development of friendship, defined by its reciprocity. You can have friendliness without friendship but not the other way round. The definition of a friend changes with age and to some extent by gender. Boys tend to interact in large activity-based groups, girls in smaller, communication-based groups. You may need to amend some activities here to be sensitive to the needs of students who struggle socially, perhaps have not had a friend and/or may be on the autistic spectrum.

Sentence Completions

- A friendly person would …
- This class/school is friendly when …
- A friend is …
- Having a friend means …

Silent Statements

Stand up and change places if you:

- have smiled at someone today
- know someone who is shy
- think people sometimes find it difficult to join in a game
- think some people don't know what to say sometimes
- believe it is OK to disagree with friends sometimes.

Activities with a Partner

Pair Shares

Find two answers to the following questions that you both agree with:

- What are reasons to have friends?
- In what ways might a friend help you feel OK?
- In what ways could you help a friend feel OK?
- If you could go anywhere with your friend, where would you like to go?
- What might spoil a friendship?
- What might mend a friendship?

Paired Interviews

Interview each other about a good friend you had. What was special about this relationship?

Interview each other about activities you enjoy with your friends. What do you like doing most?

What would you do if you wanted to join a game in the playground?

What would you do if someone wanted to join your game in the playground?

Good News   S

There are four ways of responding to good news (Gable et al., 2004):

1. Active constructive – showing real pleasure for the other person and giving them credit for any achievement.
2. Passive constructive – minimal comment such as 'that's nice'.
3. Active destructive – belittling the good news and finding something negative to say.
4. Passive destructive – ignoring it and talking about something else all together.

Model each of these ways for the whole Circle. The pairs then take it in turns to tell each other about something they have achieved that has pleased them. Each responds first in one of the last three ways and then in an active constructive way.

Discussion

What were the differences in the way you felt?

What would this mean for a relationship?

Why might someone respond in a negative or passive way?

Acrostic Poem

Give each pair some paper, and a word with five to eight letters, such as:

- friend, kindly, helping, trust, loyalty, respect

(Continued)

(Continued)

This word is written down the page with one letter on each line. The pair agrees a word or sentence beginning with each letter to make an acrostic poem about the word. For example:

Feel happy playing together

Really helps me

Important person

Every day we do things together

Nice nearly all the time

Does funny things.

Both partners have a copy of the poem. One of the pair stands in a circle facing out and their partner faces in. Everyone in the outer Circle takes three steps to their right so they are facing another partner. Both share their poems. This continues until they have been around the Circle reading their poems and hearing several others.

Extension Activity

Try doing these poems as a rap.

Whole Circle Activities

Friendly Questions and Talking Topics

Ask students in pairs to decide what a friendly question might be and how they might feel about it. They then complete these sentences:

- A friendly question is when …
- When someone asks us a friendly question we feel …

The Circle brainstorms topics for today. These might include holidays, TV programs, sporting events, things to do with school, weather, food or festivals. Once students understand what might be a second question after asking 'how are you?', they are ready for the next game.

Speed Dating

Students stand in pairs in concentric circles – one facing in and one facing out. The game starts by pairs saying to each other: 'How are you today?' They then ask one question that could be asked of anyone in the class, such as: 'What did you watch on TV last night?' 'What did you do at the weekend?' When both have had a turn, the outer circle takes three paces to the left and faces another partner to repeat the activity.

(Continued)

(Continued)

Extension Discussions

What sorts of questions are good ones to ask?

What sorts of questions encourage people to talk?
  Facilitators may need to explain the difference between open and closed questions.

Guess the Answer

Students mill around in the middle of the Circle. At a given signal they partner with someone near them. The teacher calls out a statement and each person has to guess whether or not this is true for their partner. Examples are:

- This person likes broccoli.
- This person is the eldest/youngest in their family.
- This person has broken a bone in their body.
- This person has read all of the Harry Potter books.

Once they have guessed, the person says whether or not it is true. They then repeat in another pair with another question.

Beware Crocodiles

Each pair has a large sheet of newspaper. They walk around together until the leader calls out: 'Beware crocodiles'. They put the paper on the floor to make an island and stand on it. They have to stay there for a count of five. They then fold the paper in half and walk around again. Each time the paper gets folded again until it is so small that pairs have to decide how they are going to stay on the island best. If a pair loses their balance and falls into the 'billabong' before they have got to five, they have been attacked by crocodiles and are 'out'. They return to a seat in the Circle. The winner is the pair that manages to stay on their island longest. This game is also an energizer.

Warmer ... Louder

A volunteer leaves the room and an item (treasure) is hidden. The group decides on a familiar song – the closer the person gets to the treasure the louder the song becomes, and when they move away it becomes softer.

Variations

Saying 'hotter', 'warmer', 'cooler', 'colder'
Clapping, whistling, humming.

Snowball Fight

Each pupil has a piece of A5 paper. On this they write the quality they most like in a friend. Everyone screws up their paper into a ball. At the count of five, each one throws their 'snowball' across the circle. The paper must stay within the circle, not be thrown outside. Participants pick up a snowball and throw it again. This continues for up to 30 seconds. Then at a signal everyone keeps the last 'snowball' they picked up. Each student opens this up in turn and reads what is written inside.

Secret Friend

Each participant puts their name on a piece of paper or lolly-stick. The paper is folded into four and placed in a container, preferably a cloth bag so it is impossible to see inside. Each person takes out a name. That student is their 'secret friend' for the week. During this time they do some things in school that make that person feel good. These could be brainstormed in advance.

Extension Activities

The next week a Sentence Completion could be: 'I felt good this week because …' or Silent Statements:

- Stand up and change places if you found out who your secret friend was.
- Stand up and change places if your week was especially nice.

Spoon Race

(Have a dustpan and brush ready, and if you are using water this activity is best done outside.)

Teams of about five sit in a line one behind the other. Each person has a plastic teaspoon. The person at the back has a container of water, sand, lentils or other 'spoonable' material. At a given signal they take a spoonful and pass it into the teaspoon of the second person in the line and so on, going into every teaspoon until it reaches the person at the other end who pours it into a container such as an egg cup. The winning team is the one who has the most in their front container at the end of 5 minutes or manages to fill the container.

Extension Discussions

How can teams encourage each other?

Does it help the team if people get angry with someone who has a spill?

Basket of Compliments

Have a basket full of coloured scarves. These represent compliments. First the facilitator, then the students take out a scarf and give it to another student saying – 'I would like to compliment … on his (or her) …'.

(Continued)

(Continued)

Compliments can be related to:

- what people do
- ways people behave
- qualities people have.

Pupils may begin with the way their classmates look or what they have – this will change as they begin to understand the broader range of compliments available.

Small Group Activities

Little Miss or Mr

(This game is based on the well-known children's books.)

Each small group is given the name of a Little Miss or Little Mr, such as Little Miss Generous, Little Mr Gentle, all describing a personal quality one might want in a friend. The idea is to draw this character so the rest of the Circle might be able to guess who they are. The group can offer ideas to the person who is drawing or writing. It can include what they would say or do.

Silent Construction

Each group is given some construction materials in a plastic bag. They do not open this but discuss and decide what they are going to make. After 2 minutes they take out the pieces and make their model in silence. Each group does a 'show and tell' to the Circle and talks about who did what and how they made decisions.

Variations

Simple jigsaw puzzles.

Make the tallest building that will stand up, using cardboard, straws, newspaper and sticky tape.

Make a get well card or congratulations card for someone.

Fancy Dress

Give groups some newspaper, ribbons, any scrap material available, sticky tape, felt pens, stapler and scissors. One person volunteers to be the partygoer. The group has 3 minutes to decide what character they will be going as and another 7 minutes to make the outfit. Each group then shows off the partygoer wearing their creation. This can be a lot of fun!

Ask students to report back on how they worked together and how they felt at the end.

Scavenger Hunt

This activity takes place over a week and helps students establish relationships with others and take responsibility as part of a group.

Group of about four or five are all given the same list of about 12–15 items, such as:

- the make and number plate of a red car
- a postcard from a capital city anywhere in the world
- a picture of a blue tongued lizard
- a tiny screwdriver
- a recording of Irish music
- a striped scarf
- a pair of black and white dice
- a piece of rope tied with a reef knot
- a photograph of the group
- a cake made by at least two of the group
- a European stamp
- something growing.

In the first Circle the group decides how they are going to collect the items, who does what, and how they will communicate about how the hunt is going. The following week each group does a 'show and tell', talks about what they did, how it went and the skills they used to get to their goal.

Newspaper Game

Each team is given a newspaper in the wrong order, with some pages upside down. The teams are given 2 minutes to decide how they are going to work together to put the paper in the right order. At a given signal they get to work – the first team to hold up the completed paper wins.

Feedback: How did the groups organize themselves? Did everyone have a role to play?

Variation

Choose different leaders.

Choose only one person who can speak.

Instant Treasure Hunt

The Circle is divided into groups of five or six, who sit together. The facilitator stands in the middle of the circle and calls out: 'Bring me ...'. Here are some suggestions:

- a pair of shoes that don't match
- a piece of jewellery
- a picture of a black cat
- someone who has the same letter in both their first and last names

(Continued)

(Continued)

- the oldest person in the group giving the youngest one a piggy back
- something worn inside out
- a handstand
- a smile.

The team who gets there first with each item wins a point – the first team to score five wins. If two or more people from the same team arrive with the object the team loses a point so the team has to decide whose turn it is to be the 'giver'.

Body Letters

The facilitator calls out a letter of the alphabet and the group makes themselves into that shape. Teams can do this upright or on the floor, whichever is easiest. Then get the whole class to make a word with the same number of letters as groups.

Discussions

How did everyone do that?

What worked, what would they do differently next time?

Who wanted to tell everyone what to do?

Who wanted to be told what to do?

Did people build on one another's ideas?

Variations

Do this using sign language only.

Make it into a race or making the neatest letter.

Collective Categories

Three volunteers stand as a team in the middle of the Circle. A leader seated in the Circle is given a ball to be passed around when the game begins. The facilitator calls out a group name and the team shout out as many words in that category as they can before the ball gets all the way round to the leader, who calls 'STOP'. Categories can be:

- animals
- vegetables
- things you would find in a bathroom
- ball sports
- things to sit on
- musical instruments
- forms of transport.

The group of three is asked if it helped with ideas to hear what others said. Give several teams a turn.

Alphabet Lists

Each team is given about 12 categories on paper. The leader calls out a letter of the alphabet and each team has to write down something in each category that begins with that letter within a given time limit, such as 3 minutes. If this is run as a competition you might give one point for getting an item in that category and an extra point for something that is different from everyone else. This encourages creativity.

Think Again – Uses For...

Give each team an everyday object such as a coat hanger, a table or a glove and ask them to identify as many different uses for it as they can. They can be as imaginative as they like, including making it a different size or made from a different material. This activity supports the development of the divergent thinking critical to innovation.

Rights and Responsibilities

Although making ethical decisions can be complex it is mostly related to what is most fair. Copy the table below and cut up so each right and responsibility is on a different piece of paper. Small groups match up the rights with the responsibilities. Now ask groups to see if they can put these in order with the most important first. There are no right or wrong answers, but the group needs to give reasons for their choice.

Table 9.1   Our Rights and responsibilities

Our Rights	Our Responsibilities
Not to be accused of something I haven't done	To check with people what matters to them
Not to be made fun of because I am different in some way	To listen to what other people have to say, not ignore, interrupt or put them down
To be treated fairly	To accept and celebrate that we are all different
To be listened to	Not to accuse others
	To be honest and own up when I do something wrong
To have a say in what concerns me	To have courage and stand up for others when you see them being treated badly
For others to stand up for me	To be fair to others

 Photocopiable:
Circle Solutions for Student Wellbeing © Sue Roffey, 2014 (SAGE)

True or False

In small groups the students discuss one of these statements at a time and decide whether they think it is true or false, or 'it depends', giving their reasons for their answer to the Circle:

(Continued)

(Continued)

- It is always bad to fail a test.
- If you don't join in with cyber-bullying you might get targeted.
- Some people are just born bad.
- It would be great to be famous.
- There is no point in worrying.
- It's not what happens to you that matters most – it's how you deal with it.
- Only girls cry.
- We are more afraid of what we don't know than what we do know.
- Teachers should always be strict.

Fair or Unfair: What Should Happen Now?

Give the scenarios in Table 9.2 to small groups and ask them to decide what is fair or unfair. They then discuss what should happen now. Teachers could choose just one scenario for the whole Circle or give different groups different scenarios. In either case, ensure there is time for feedback.

Embedding Circle Solutions as a Tool for Wellbeing

Friends and friendship is an issue in every class but can be particularly problematic in primary school. There will be daily opportunities to encourage students to reflect on and use their Circle learning.

Growing a Tree of Friendship

This has been a successful activity in many classes. It both acknowledges pro-social behaviours but continually gives pupils ideas of what are friendly things to do and say. For less skilled students you may need to structure success experiences in the first instance.

The bare branches of a tree are drawn on the classroom wall. Children are told that they are growing their 'tree of friendship' for the class. Pupils are asked to look out for each other doing and saying especially friendly things in class and playtimes and then report back to the Circle. Identified children are given a leaf with their name on it and what they said or did – the leaf is placed on the tree that grows each week for a whole term.

Extension

Blossoms for group friendliness!

Random Acts of Kindness

There is evidence that doing things for others increases our own wellbeing. Put up a pinboard in the classroom (or even the corridor) and ask everyone to put up little thank you notes for random acts of kindness. Include adults. Ask people to also write how it made them feel. This board will become a focus of discussion. Ensure that children with special educational needs have the opportunity do things for others and be acknowledged for this – they are usually on the receiving end.

Table 9.2   Fair or unfair?

What happens?	Fair or unfair?	Do we need to change what happens – and how? If not, why not?
Timmy has been playing with the bike for a long time. Abby asks for a go but he says he hasn't finished yet.		
The plate of cookies is for all the children but some take too many so others miss out.		
There is only one book between two people. Cassie holds the book in front of her and Daniel can't see it.		
Sana cannot read yet so the teacher spends more time helping her than the other children.		
There are lots of jobs that need doing in the classroom. The teacher has made a list so that everyone has a turn.		
On the table are eight coloured pens for six children to use. Matthew has got three in his hand; he says he's using them.		
When the teacher asks the whole class a question Sam shouts out the answer.		
Monica is going to have a party. She asks all the girls in her class except for Izzy.		

Photocopiable:
Circle Solutions for Student Wellbeing © Sue Roffey, 2014 (SAGE)

Pass It On Gotcha Cards

Have five to ten Gotcha cards that say things like:

- I gotcha inviting someone into a game
- I gotcha asking how someone was today
- I gotcha giving someone a helping hand

These are not rewards but acknowledgements and are first given out by a teacher who is specific about why someone is receiving this. Once someone has been given a Gotcha card they then look out for someone showing the same friendly behaviour and pass it on. Have just one or two circulating at a time.

10

Circle Solutions for Challenging Situations

> This chapter deals with some of the difficult issues students face and the feelings that may arise from these. Some challenging situations are short-term, others on-going and part of life. Some individuals deal with one adversity, others face multiple stresses. These issues are often at the root of many of the social, emotional and behavioural outcomes manifested in school. The aims of Circle strategies in this chapter are to:
>
> - provide an opportunity to talk about challenging issues safely
> - show students that others have similar experiences and they are not alone
> - help students learn the skills involved in effective problem-solving
> - construct coping strategies
> - explore difficult feelings and how to stop these from becoming overwhelming
> - encourage students to develop collaborative solutions to problematic issues
> - reflect on individual and class responsibilities.

Young people having a hard time may be awash with negative emotion and find it difficult to concentrate, make friends, behave in pro-social ways or cooperate with teachers. These 'double whammy kids' then get into trouble, labelled in negative ways and sometimes excluded. The activities throughout this book not only promote more positive and inclusive environments for vulnerable pupils but also create opportunities to reflect on different ways of being and becoming.

Introducing Issues Safely

Individuals need to feel comfortable and safe when difficult issues are being addressed in a Circle, and teachers need to feel confident about facilitating. The use of puppets, stories and games engage students with limited personal risk. Should students become distressed in any way however, the facilitator needs to give them the opportunity to opt out or use their Circle Solutions file. It is essential to follow this up with a conversation that shows concern and, if appropriate, a referral to a suitable professional.

Puppets

Creative teachers use puppets to motivate young students to be thoughtful problem-solvers. Give puppets names and characters and make them regular visitors to the Circle. Puppets can talk with the teacher and the children about problems such as being teased or left out, not being sure about something or being frightened. The puppets ask for suggestions as to what they could do. The students can discuss the puppets' problems in small groups and give feedback in the Circle. A follow-up in the next Circle session reinforces the learning.

Stories   YMS

Stories are a useful means to engage students and stimulate discussion. These are available both in books and other media for a wide range of ages and abilities. They free up individuals to talk about issues rather than divulging personal events.

The facilitator reads a short story or shows a short film to the Circle focusing on a specific issue. These might include: being called names, being left out, cyber cruelty, life changes, losing someone you love, having a bad day, failing a test, being sick, disability, racism, family matters, fear and anxiety, peer group pressure, or natural disasters. Ideas for stimulus material are in the resource chapter.

This is followed by a paired or small group discussion with feedback to the full Circle. The following are general suggestions; some stories give rise to more specific questions.

Discussions

What did you feel hearing this story?

Did your feelings change as the story went on?

What do you think were the feelings of the characters in the story?

Without giving names, do you know anyone who might have had similar experiences?

Has this story made you think or feel differently about their situation?

What things could be done to help?

What does this story mean for our class and/or others in this school?

What did you think about the ending of the story? What might have been an alternative?

Extension Activities

YMS   Small groups act out the story and then talk about the thoughts and feelings of the characters.

YMS   Small groups make up and act out a story that is about the same issue but different from the one that has been read out.

MS   In pairs, one person takes on the role of the main character and the other interviews them about what happens in the story.

MS   Small groups make a strip cartoon of a similar situation.

MS   Each small group has a large piece of paper placed horizontally. A line is drawn across the middle from left to right. The group plots the story from the beginning on the left to the end of the right, marking the places where there were alternative decisions to be made. Choices that might have changed things for the better are written on top of the line and choices that would have made things worse are written at the bottom.

Detective

Feeling uncomfortable signals that a problem needs to be addressed. These are hypothetical situations that might make someone feel uncomfortable:

- You agreed to see a film with someone, but then get asked to a party, which would be more fun.
- You see someone bigger and older pushing and poking a child on the way to school.
- A group in the class is texting messages to someone you know saying they are ugly and a 'loser'.
- Your friend is spreading rumours about another girl which may or may not be true.
- You borrowed something from a friend and now can't find it.
- You joined in with laughing at someone, even though it really upsets them.
- Your brother lent you some money and now wants it back. You don't have it.

Pupils may have other examples.

Ask students to discuss in groups what the problem really is and brainstorm all the possible solutions. They list the positives and negatives of each, including potential consequences. The group chooses the solution they think best and give reasons. Each group reports to the Circle.

The next two activities, which we developed together, appear in more detail in Bill Hansberry and Jane Langley's excellent book *The Grab and Go Circle Time Kit for Teaching Restorative Behaviour* (2012).

Inside Outside Hurts

This activity is designed to raise awareness of emotional hurt and to think of what helps.

Explain to children that 'outside hurts' are when a part of your body is damaged even though this might be invisible, such as a headache. 'Inside hurts' are when something happens that makes you feel angry or sad.

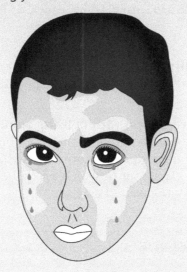

Figure 10.1 Child crying

Photocopiable:
Circle Solutions for Student Wellbeing © Sue Roffey, 2014 (SAGE)

(Continued)

(Continued)

Some things are both inside and outside hurts, for example someone kicking or hitting you. List, one at a time, a variety of 'hurts', such as a broken leg, a bump on the head, a grazed knee, being left out, laughed at or ignored. The students call out if each is an outside or an inside hurt.

Talk to the students about how our bodies sometimes hurt to tell us that we need to pay attention and look after ourselves. There are things that help with outside hurts: plasters, ointments or pills, etc. The most effective thing, though, is time. Sometimes we need to pay attention to inside hurts as well. They might help us to understand what is important, what we need to do or how other people might feel.

Ask the children to talk to each other in pairs about the sorts of things that might help with 'inside hurts'. What has helped them not feel so bad? The pairs decide on two things, and give feedback to the group. Make the connection with time.

A picture of a child crying is placed in the centre of the circle.

Pair Share

Talk about what might have made this person cry. Think of two reasons – an outside hurt and an inside hurt.

The teacher lists these hurts into two columns. Mix children up so they have different partners. Each pair is given an inside hurt and an outside hurt from the list generated. For each hurt they complete the following sentence.

If someone was hurt by ... they would feel ... because ...

Helping with Hurts

Children work in small groups. They are asked to talk about what they have found has helped them with outside hurts. What was done and who helped? Divide these up into family, friends and people whose job it is to help.

They are then asked to talk about what has helped them or other people with inside hurts. What did they do and what did other people do that made them feel better?

Specific Challenging Issues

Bullying

No student should have to deal with bullying alone, including racial and sexual taunts. There is increasing recognition that the continued existence of bullying depends on whether it is condoned by others. The following activities support the development of a safe classroom in which everyone takes responsibility for what happens.

Silent Statements
Stand up and change places if:

- you know there is bullying in this school
- you have seen bullying happen
- you have heard put-downs in this class

- you have felt sorry for someone who was bullied
- you want to feel safe in school
- you have ever been sorry for something you have said or done.

Sentence Completions

- Bullying is when ...
- Someone would feel bullied if ...
- Watching someone being bullied would make you feel ...
- A person who bullies others might feel ...
- Bullying affects everyone because ...
- People bully others because ...

Recipe for a Safe and Happy Class

Small groups decide what would go into their recipe. Some ingredients are things you hear, some are what you see and others are feelings. Young pupils might need help to write the ingredients down or know what is available in the store cupboard!

- smiles
- friends
- playing together
- kindness
- helping
- saying hello
- feeling comfortable
- laughing
- talking
- making a space to let someone in

Extension Discussions

How much of each ingredient might you need?

What things might spoil your recipe for a safe and happy class?

How could you stop this getting into the mix?

What actions will we all take to ensure this class is safe and happy?

Confidence Cake

A similar group activity is for students to devise a recipe for a confidence cake. What helps build confidence? How would you mix these ingredients? How would you cook your cake and what would you decorate it with? Students write the recipe and draw a picture of their cake to show the Circle. The facilitator points out which ingredients are factors within someone and what is needed from others.

Taking Care of Teddy

Each small group is given a soft toy, such as a teddy. They are told the toy's name and that the toy is a bit scared of coming to school because people might be unkind. The group talk about what they could do to make sure that the teddy was safe and happy. Feed back to the Circle.

P-Charts   MS

Bullying is picking on someone (or deliberately ignoring them), in a situation in which there is a power imbalance. The behaviour is persistent (happens regularly) and prolonged (goes on over time).

The groups are given a piece of paper divided into four, with a heading in each square:

- Picking On
- Power Imbalance
- Persistent
- Prolonged

Each group is given the same scenario, either one of those below or another devised for the class. In each square they fill in the details of what this means for this situation. When they have done this, they take a second piece of paper divided up into squares with the words:

- Prevent
- Protect
- Plan of Action
- Appraise

They brainstorm ideas about how this situation might be prevented in the first place and what might be done to protect the person being bullied. In 'Plan of Action' they decide on the best options and who will do what. The final square outlines how they would evaluate how well the plan is working.

Scenarios

- A student with learning difficulties is encouraged by a couple of other students to do silly or unkind things out of the sight of the teacher. He thinks they are being friendly and likes making them laugh.
- One girl in the class likes to have control. She targets another girl and tells her friends not to have anything to do with her. This girl is sneered at or ignored and nothing she can do makes it any better. She is increasingly miserable and doesn't want to go to school.
- One boy has a stutter. Most days others copy him for a laugh. He doesn't think it's funny.
- One girl is particularly good at maths. A couple of 'friends' asked her to help them with their homework. At first they are really nice, but when she becomes reluctant to do their work for them they say they won't be her friend any more. She doesn't know what to do.

(Continued)

(Continued)

- A teacher seems to have taken a dislike to a particular student. The pupil is not asked to contribute nor receives any positive comment on their work or effort. The teacher makes occasional sarcastic or belittling comments.
- A boy is having a hard time at home and easily gets upset. Others wind him up so he loses his temper. He then gets into trouble from teachers.

Extension Activity

In the centre of the Circle, role-play the characters in the scenario:

- the person being bullied
- the person leading the bullying
- those joining in
- bystanders who watch
- those who defend

The first time, play the scene as described; the second time, intervene to support the person being bullied. Debrief by talking about the feelings of each character, both at the time of the 'incident' and afterwards.

Silence or Support – Bystander Intervention

Google the 'un-making of a bully' or 'the price of silence anti-bullying video' or any other clip that is suitable for your class and that shows how bystanders might intervene. Show the film to your students and ask them to discuss this. Questions might include:

- Have you seen something like this in school?
- Why do you think this behaviour happens?
- What do you think of the person who intervenes?
- What helped this intervention be effective?
- What are three things you have learnt from this video?

Cyber-bullying

What If This Happened to You?

(Taken from Roffey, 2011)

Ask for volunteers to role-play this scenario for the whole Circle.

Ella:	You are in a new school and haven't made friends yet. You miss your mates a lot. You are pleased that Chi and Brianna are spending some time with you.
Chi and Brianna:	You don't get on so well with others in your class. You are interested in Ella when she arrives and try to find out everything you can about her.

(Continued)

(Continued)

Scene 1:   Conversation between Ella, Chi and Brianna finding out about each other.

Scene 2:   Chi explains to Brianna that it would be a real laugh to put Ella's picture up on Facebook and let everyone know something about her, including some really personal information. Brianna isn't so sure but goes along with Chi as she is her friend.

Scene 3:   Ella reads what has been written about her. It isn't nice.

Scene 4:   Ella comes into school and asks Chi and Brianna why they did that. Chi and Brianna attack her for not being 'fun' to be around. Ella is left stranded.

Facilitator asks the actors:

- What did you feel about being Ella?
- Did you feel comfortable being Chi or Brianna?
- How did you encourage each other?

Facilitator divides students into small groups who discuss the following:

- How would you feel if this happened to you?
- What might have stopped the cyber-bullying?
- What do you think should happen now?

Cyber Virus

The cyber-bullying virus can cause great damage. Someone carrying the virus might start to spread it with a text saying something nasty, such as …

- No one likes you. Everyone hates you.
- You are ugly, fat, a loser, a creep, stupid.

This virus is very contagious. Every post, text or email spreads it further. When it appears on Facebook, more and more people get involved and become carriers. It becomes 'cool to be cruel' and people fear that if they don't join in it might be their turn next.

The person who is being attacked has nowhere to go – the virus is in their phone, computer, at school, at home, on the street – everywhere. Some young people are very badly affected by the cyber-bullying virus.

The agents that promote this dangerous virus are:

- hate, anger, envy, power, peer pressure.

Like any disease, there are some powerful antidotes. Antidotes to the cyber-bullying virus are:

- courage, compassion, kindness, collaboration, conversation.

Small Group Activity

Students are divided into small groups to discuss the following: Has anyone had flu? Did you deserve to get the flu virus? Does anyone deserve to be attacked by the

(Continued)

(Continued)

cyber-bullying virus? How would it feel to be attacked? How would it affect your life? Could a cyber-bullying attack be fatal?

They talk about the agents of cyber-bullying. Which is the strongest of these and how does it show itself? The groups then talk about how each of the antidotes might work. What would you see, what would you hear? How would each of them help stop the virus from spreading? Which is the strongest antidote? Do you need more than one antidote to stop the virus? How might they work together?

Extension Activities

Each person in the Circle is given a role as one of the agents or one of the antidotes. These get together and talk about what they would do to spread or contain the virus.

One person volunteers to play the victim. For each attack one or more of the antidotes goes into action.

Working in small groups, students make one or more of the following:

- photo collage of positive texts and messages to counter cyber-bullying
- T-shirt or badge designs to show that you are against cyber-bullying
- posters to put around the school with five things someone can do if they are being cyber-bullied. They need to know they are not alone and that support and help are available.

Loss

Loss is a serious issue for many young people and at the root of strong emotions. These activities address the universality of this experience. There are some excellent programs available to help students with change and loss.

Silent Statements
Stand up and change places if:

- you have ever moved house
- have lived in another country
- the team you support has ever lost a match
- someone has taken something that belonged to you or your family
- a family pet has died
- you know someone who has lost an important person in their lives.

Loss and Losing   YMS

In small groups, students make a list of everything that people might lose, from losing a game or a possession to losing an important person. Loss is not only about death but someone disappearing from your life in other ways.

- What are all the feelings you might experience when this happens?
- Do the circumstances of the loss make a difference to your feelings?
- What has helped people come to terms with a loss? Make a list.

Celebrating a Life

In small groups, discuss how you might celebrate someone's life, or an animal you had loved and lost. Be sensitive to individual situations here.

Make a poster with drawings and words.

What might you want to put in a memory box to help remember them?

Losing someone at school and loss of trust happens at any age – how the following activities are introduced needs to be appropriate for the level of understanding of the pupils involved.

Losing Someone at School

Without going into details or breaching confidentiality, the facilitator – who could be a counsellor alongside the teacher – speaks to the Circle about what happened. Facts are usually easier to deal with than imagination. It is useful to acknowledge the range of emotions that may accompany this announcement. These include:

- shock
- sadness
- emptiness
- anger
- numbness
- confusion
- fear
- indifference.

Not everyone will feel the same. How individuals feel depends on many things, including how well they knew the person, the circumstances of the death and what else is happening in their own life.

Ask students to talk to each other in pairs about what support people might need at this time. What, if anything, do they need for themselves and what could they do for others? The facilitator might then choose one or more of the following activities, perhaps leaving this for later Circle sessions.

In pairs, talk about the person and in what ways they might be missed.

In small groups plan a memorial Circle for the person. Each group decides what they will do.

Loss of Trust

Loss of trust happens when someone lies, breaks confidences, talks behind your back, takes things or lets you down. This can be a class concern as well as an individual one and difficult to address. These activities help to do so without accusation and blame.

Sentence Completions
- Trusting someone means ...
- Keeping confidences means ...
- Being honest means ...
- It is easier to trust someone who ...
- I would feel let down by someone if ...
- We need to trust people in this class because ...

Pair Shares

Trust means different things to different people. Interview each other and find out what it means for them. How important is trust in a friendship?

What happens to friendships when trust is broken? Can it be mended? How might trust be restored?

A Trick for Trust

Each group has two pieces of paper. Each represents the same classroom. In one trust is present, and in the other it is absent. Draw Y charts for each scenario – what do people say, what do people do, what does everyone feel?
  Discuss in the whole Circle:

- Which class is a better place to be?
- What can we do to encourage trust in this class?

Conflict

Conflict is an inevitable part of life: people see things differently, want different things and have different priorities. It is how it is managed that matters. Conflict that is not managed well can lead to feelings of hate, revenge and violence.

Silent Statements

Stand up and change places if:

- you have ever felt that something was very unfair
- you have argued over who was right about something
- you thought you had a right to something and so did someone else
- you have felt that your viewpoint was not listened to or respected
- someone has wanted you to do something you did not want to do
- you have ever regretted something you said or did
- you have felt stuck in a conflict situation.

Swapping Sides

Each pair is given a conflict situation such as:

- someone accusing another of cheating in a game
- one person deriding the religion of the other
- two people wanting the same thing
- someone labelling the other person in a negative way.

They each take up one role and begin a conversation. After 2 minutes the facilitator stops the conversation and asks the pair to swap seats. They then start arguing from the other person's position.

(Continued)

(Continued)

Discussions

How did they feel in the different roles?
  Did they begin to understand that there were two sides to a conflict?
  What happened that made the conflict worse? What helped?

Conflict Conversations

Each pair is given a conflict situation. An example could be:

- A young person queues up to get an ice cream. As they are leaving with the ice cream in their hand another person runs into them, not looking where they are going. The ice cream is knocked to the ground. The first person screams abuse and the second takes offence and starts to threaten violence.

Each person takes one of the roles and is given 1 minute without the other interrupting to give their view of the situation and what they think happened. Then each person is given 30 seconds to say what they feel but does not blame the other. This means a sentence beginning 'I felt ... when you ... ', rather than 'You made me ... '. Each person says what they would want as an outcome. Both partners brainstorm solutions and choose one.

Flight, Fight or Doing It Right? MS

Give small groups these actions and statements and ask them to divide them into three piles: one a passive flight response, one an aggressive fight response and the other assertive:

- 'You made me do that'
- Complain about someone behind their back
- Walk a different way home to avoid someone
- 'I feel it's unfair to ask me for help when I'm watching my favourite TV program'
- 'You have no idea what you're talking about'
- Shout and scream
- Go silent
- 'When you yell at me, it's hard to listen to what you're saying'
- Agree with someone for the sake of peace and quiet
- Ask someone to let you know the day before when plans have been changed
- 'I'm just telling you ...'
- 'When I have something important to tell you, I feel upset if you don't listen to me'

Extension Discussions

What actions/statements are more likely to resolve a conflict? Which will add to the conflict?

What feelings are likely for each of these actions/statements for both parties?

Feelings That Challenge

The main aim of the following activities is to reflect on ways to limit the damage that negative feelings can do to individuals and to others.

Anger

Anger can be related to many things, including loss, attacks on self-esteem and injustice. These activities help students to understand the many roots of anger and ways of expressing their anger safely.

Silent Statements

Stand up and change places if you have:

- seen someone be angry because of something someone said
- seen someone be angry because they jumped to the wrong conclusion
- seen someone be angry because they have been left out of something
- seen someone be angry because they felt they were hurt or treated badly
- been angry because things didn't go the way you wanted
- been angry because you saw other people being treated badly
- been angry and not really known why
- had times in your life when you have felt like crying with frustration
- been angry because you have lost something or someone
- been angry at the 'wrong person'
- been able to keep in control of your anger
- sometimes let your anger be in control of you
- been angry about some of the things that are happening in your world.

Pair Shares

- What things make you both angry?
- What have you done with those angry feelings?
- In which ways might anger be useful?

Ready, Steady, Stop

Give each small group three body-outlines. The first is headed 'Green – all calm'. The second is headed 'Orange – on the alert'. The third is headed 'Red – danger zone'. Write the bodily responses for each level: calm is when things are going your way, orange is when a potential threat appears and red is when the body is fired up to respond. Threats to a sense of self mean that the body gets ready for either flight or fight. Anger is likely to lead to a fight response.

Discussion

What can you do when you feel yourself getting angry?

What can you do to show that you are angry that does not get you into trouble or make things worse?

Four Corners

YMS

Mark corners of the room with the colours red, blue, green, yellow.

- Red: Be verbally or physically abusive
- Blue: Bottle it all up and seethe inside
- Yellow: Wait and see
- Green: Do something else.

Students are given a scenario and go to the corner that shows what they would do. The following are examples, but students could come up with many others:

- someone pushing in front of them in a queue
- being mildly insulted/teased
- being rejected/told to '---- off'
- their family is insulted
- someone not looking where they are going and barging into them
- someone taking something without asking

Discussions

Does it matter who was doing these things?
What about the circumstances?
What are the 'other things' that someone might do in a stressful situation?
What might this mean in the future for you?

Worry

Worry Warts

YMS

Some anxieties get bigger if you keep picking at them but fade away if you deal with them effectively. Discuss in pairs what would 'grow' worries and what would shrink them. Here are some examples:

- there's something nasty under the bed!
- you will forget something important
- you will fail an exam
- you will lose something
- you will do something foolish
- you might have upset a friend

Feed back one thing each that helps worries get smaller.

The Last Straw

MS

Give small groups a pile of thin coloured sticks (straws) about six inches long. These are piled into a heap. Each person takes one stick from the pile in turn. The aim is to prevent all the other sticks collapsing. How many sticks can the group retrieve before this happens?

(Continued)

(Continued)

Discussions

Often many negative or difficult things happen before you get to that 'last straw', when you feel that you can no longer 'hold it all together'.

- Can you give examples of how things pile up?
- How can you tell if someone is getting very stressed? What are the signs?
- What might stop stress building up or increase the resources to cope?
- The group feeds back their ideas to the Circle.

Feeling Blue

Sadness and Depression

Ask for two volunteers to stand in the middle of the Circle – one to represent sadness and one to represent depression. Ask the Circle to say how each might stand, how each face might look. The two actors comply with instructions.

What might have happened to each person (sadness is usually a response to specific events, depression might not be)?

Can you usually tell if someone is sad?
Can you always tell if someone is depressed?
What is the difference between the two?
What does the sad person need? (comfort, a good friend, time)
What does the depressed person need? (more specialist help)

Silent Statements
Stand up and change places if:

- you have ever had a day in which nothing seemed to go right
- you have ever felt like staying in bed all day
- you know someone who is sad and upset about something that is going on in their life
- you know someone who has recovered from a difficult time and is now doing well.

Managing Mountains

In pairs, each student draws a mountain and a small person at the bottom of it. This mountain represents the biggest challenge that the student has faced. Each student talks to the other about the qualities that help them to manage the mountains in their life. Do they see themselves as getting through it, over it or around it?

Feed back to the group. Each student says one quality that helped the other person but not their story.

Embedding Circle Solutions as a Tool for Wellbeing

School policies on social justice, equal opportunities and safety need to be clear and effective.

It is helpful for all adults to be aware of the multiple issues that may affect student learning and behaviour and use relational/emotionally literate responses that maintain high expectations but do not exacerbate difficulties.

Once there is a sense of connectedness, develop restorative approaches to behaviour so students understand what is meant by 'doing sorry' rather than just 'saying sorry'.

Appendix 1

Twelve Dimensions for Learning Relationships and Promoting Wellbeing: Lesson Content and Congruent School Context

	SEL dimension	Content	Context
1	Self-awareness • Being and becoming	Identification of values, beliefs, strengths and goals	Clarity of school values, vision, priorities and direction A focus on the wellbeing of the whole child
2	Emotional awareness and knowledge • The biology and psychology of emotion • Personal triggers • Social construction	Understanding the range of emotions and how they are experienced within the body. Awareness of personal, social and cultural influences on feelings	Emotional 'tone' of the school and how this is demonstrated Awareness of the influences on this development
3	Emotional skills • Regulation • Expression • Coping and resilience	Dealing with and regulating negative emotion Acceptable expression of feelings Knowing what sustains emotional wellbeing and promotes resilience	Awareness of adult models of emotional literacy Communication of expectations – validating feelings but not accepting hurtful words and actions Staff wellbeing
4	Shared humanity • How do we position others in our world?	Appreciating uniqueness for the self and others Valuing diversity while seeking what is shared Inclusive belonging	Celebration of diversity Actively addressing racism, sexism and homophobia Inclusive policies for students with special needs
5	Interpersonal skills • Skills needed to establish and maintain positive relationships with others	Exploring the meaning and practice of relational values Positive communication skills Collaboration and cooperation	Positive teacher–student relationships Staff collegiality Collaborative pedagogies Positive communication practices Support systems

(Continued)

(Continued)

	SEL dimension	Content	Context
6	Situational skills • Tuning into the emotional context	Empathy Reading, interpreting and tuning into emotions in situations Not pre-judging Awareness of timing	Taking account of emotions in situations of challenge, change, failure and loss Flexibility and appropriate responsiveness in highly charged situations
7	Leadership	Goal setting Taking initiative and responsibility Confidence Dealing with peer pressure Empowering others	Communication of vision Acknowledging and trusting others 'Walking the talk' Avoiding blame Being in charge, but not controlling others Student and staff voice
8	Promoting the positive • Strengths and solutions approach	Optimism Gratitude Humour Perspective Identification of strengths in self and others	Identifying what is going well and ways to increase this Working with the positive Positive behaviour policies Pedagogies for fun, meaning and engagement
9	Conflict and confrontation • Dealing well with relational difficulties	Negotiation Compromise Appropriate assertiveness Problem-solving skills	Pre-empting potential conflict Appropriate use of authority De-escalating confrontation Addressing conflict actively Anti-bullying policies
10	Repair and restoration • Mending damage in relationships and restoring community	Acknowledging hurt Willingness to compromise Responding to repair overtures Action to repair harm – doing 'sorry'	Restorative approaches to behaviour Mistakes as part of learning for all Policies of re-integration for excluded students
11	Ethics and integrity • Human rights dimensions of SEL	Honesty, trust Consistency Ethical decision-making Focus on human rights	Core values in social justice Congruence between values, policies and practices Authenticity
12	Spirituality • Seeking meaning in life	Developing a philosophy for life beyond the self Environmental responsibility	Educational philosophy focused on the whole child in all dimensions of development alongside community/global awareness and contribution to others

This table (now amended and further developed) was first published in Roffey, 2010.

Appendix 2
Games Index

Name	Who for?	Description	SEL Dimension(s)	YMS	Ch.	Page
A Trick for Trust	Small Groups	Y charts to look at when trust is present or not	7	MS	10	105
Absent But Not Forgotten	Small Groups	To support students away from school	4, 5	YMS	8	78
Acrostic Poem	Pairs	Thinking about friendship values	5	MS	9	84
Active Listening Skills	Pairs	What it feels like to be listened to (or not)	5	MS	5	43
Affirmations	Whole Circle	Being and becoming, reflecting on who to be	1, 12	MS	3	29
Aladdin's Lamp	Pairs	Three wishes – to have, to do, to be	1, 11, 12	YMS	4	35
All Change	Pairs	Promoting attention and observational skills	1, 5	MS	5	43
Alphabet Lists	Small Groups	Using everyone's ideas	4, 5	YMS	9	91
Amygdala Moments	Small Groups	The role of the amygdala in an emotional hijack	2	MS	6	57
Angry Alex	Whole Circle	What triggers certain emotions	2	YM	6	55
At the Movies	Small Groups	Conveying situations without words	5, 6	M	5	48
Autographs	Whole Circle	For students who do not know each other yet	4, 5	MS	3	24

(Continued)

(Continued)

Name	Who for?	Description	SEL Dimension(s)	YMS	Ch.	Page
Basket of Compliments	Whole Circle	Noticing the positives in others	5, 8	YM	9	87
Beware Crocodiles	Whole Circle	Cooperation and laughter	5, 8	YM	9	86
Birthday Lines	Whole Circle	Communication without words	5	YMS	5	45
Body Letters	Small Groups	Working together to construct a letter	4, 5, 7	YM	9	90
Bucket Fillers	Whole Circle	Awareness of what raises or depletes resources	2, 3, 5	YMS	6	56
Bunnies	Whole Circle	A fun way of greeting each other	4, 8	YMS	3	23
Catch Me If You Can	Whole Circle	Reading faces	3	YM	6	54
Catching Feelings	Small Groups	How emotions infect others	2	MS	6	59
Celebrating a Life	Small Groups	Creative activity to help with talking	4, 5, 6	YMS	10	104
Chaser	Whole Circle	Energizer, inclusion and getting to know names	5, 8	YM	3	24
Check-in	Whole Circle	Communicating how you are feeling today	2	YMS	3	23
Circle Knot	Whole Circle	Group problem-solving	5, 7	MS	8	73
Clapping Rhythms	Whole Circle	Paying attention – listening skills	5, 7	YM	5	44
Class Wall of Strength	Whole Circle	Strengths identification for a whole class	4, 8	M	4	39
Class Web	Whole Circle	We all belong and it matters that we are here	4	YMS	8	73
Collages	Small Groups	Creative activity to talk about feelings	3	MS	6	59
Collective Categories	Small Groups	Sparking ideas together	1, 5	YMS	9	90
Confidence Cake	Small Groups	What helps build confidence?	1, 11	MS	10	99
Conflict Conversations	Pairs	Bare outline of a restorative conversation	10	MS	10	106
Cyber Virus	Small Groups	The agents and antidotes to cyber-bullying	2, 11	MS	10	102

Name	Who for?	Description	SEL Dimension(s)	YMS	Ch.	Page
Detective	Small Groups	Addressing uncomfortable situations	1, 6, 9, 11	YMS	10	97
Dream Time	Pairs	Identifying futures	1, 7	YMS	4	36
Dreams and Nightmares	Pairs	You can have feelings about what is not real	2	MS	6	53
Encouragement	Pairs	Encouraging conversation and participation	5	MS	5	43
Faces	Whole Circle	Not everyone feels the same in a situation	2, 6	Y	6	54
Fair or Unfair?	Small Groups	What should happen to make things fair?	9, 10, 11	YM	9	92
Fancy Dress	Small Groups	What to wear and how to make it, creativity	5, 7	MS	9	88
Feelings in Pictures	Pairs	Drawing how we feel and others tuning in	2, 6	YMS	6	52
Flight, Fight or Doing It Right?	Small Groups	The value of appropriate assertiveness	9	MS	10	106
Flour Cake	Whole Circle	Every action matters – promoting laughter	5, 8	YM	8	74
Four Corners	Whole Circle	Alternative responses to difficult situations	2, 3	YMS	10	108
Fox and Rabbit	Whole Circle	Energizer and group cooperation	5, 9	YM	8	73
Freeze Frame	Small Groups	Emotional management	3	MS	6	57
Friendly Questions and Talking Topics	Whole Circle	Knowing what to say after 'How are you?'	5	YMS	9	85
Future Map	Pairs	Exploring possible futures	7, 12	MS	4	36
Future World	Small Groups	Reflecting on values in being future parents	1, 12	S	4	38
Give Us a Clue	Small Groups	Empathy with those who struggle to read	6, 1	S	8	77

(Continued)

Name	Who for?	Description	SEL Dimension(s)	YMS	Ch.	Page
Going On Camp	Whole Circle	Whole Circle support	5, 9	YMS	5	46
Good News	Pairs	Different ways of responding to good news	5	S	9	84
Growing a Tree of Friendship	Whole Circle	Acknowledging friendly actions and words	4, 5	YM	9	92
Guess the Answer	Whole Circle	Guessing and finding out about each other	5	YMS	9	86
Guess the Feeling	Small Groups	Building an emotion vocabulary	3	MS	6	60
Guess the Leader	Whole Circle	Focusing attention and leading a group	5, 7	YMS	5	46
Guessing Good At	Whole Circle	Identifying strengths in others and owning yours	1, 4	YMS	4	34
Happy, Sad, Excited, Scared	Whole Circle	Mix-up activity showing strengths of emotion	3	YMS	6	54
Have You Filled a Bucket Today?	Whole Circle	Taking action to support others	2, 3, 6	YMS	6	61
Headlines	Small Groups	Exploring the positives in negative situations	8, 9	MS	7	65
Heard You!	Whole Circle	Focus, attention and listening skills	5	YMS	5	45
Hello Goodbye	Whole Circle	Learning different greetings and farewells	5	YM	3	22
Helping with Hurts	Small Groups	Identifying sources of support to promote resilience	2, 3, 4, 10	Y	10	98
Here Be Monsters	Whole Circle	Group support to negotiate obstacles	4, 5, 9	YM	8	74
History and Culture	Pairs or Small Groups	Cultural impacts on feelings such as pride	2	MS	6	53
I Feel It Here!	Small Groups	The bodily sensations of different emotions	2	YMS	6	57
I See You	Whole Circle	Practising eye contact	5	YM	5	46
In the Dark	Small Groups	Trust and empathy with visual impairment	6, 11	YMS	8	79

Name	Who for?	Description	SEL Dimension(s)	YMS	Ch.	Page
In the Manner of the Word	Whole Circle	Representing and reading emotions, energizer	2, 3, 6	MS	6	55
Inside Outside Hurts	Pairs	Understanding physical and emotional hurt	2, 6	Y	10	97
Instant Treasure Hunt	Small Groups	Sharing responsibility to find items	4, 5, 7	YMS	9	89
Internet Biography Searches	Pairs or Small Groups	Identifying the value of strengths in other lives	1, 11, 12	S	4	33
Jump To It!	Whole Circle	Energizer that identifies what every child needs	11	YM	8	72
Kim's Game	Pairs	Visual attention and collaboration	5, 9	YMS	5	44
Life Map	Pairs	Major events and what really matters	1, 11, 12	MS	4	36
Little Miss or Mr	Small Groups	The personification of friendly qualities	5	YM	9	88
Loss and Losing	Small Groups	Loss happens to everyone – what helps?	2	YMS	10	103
Mad, Sad, Bad and Glad	Whole Circle	Categorizing and talking about different feelings	2, 3	YMS	6	55
Managing Mountains	Pairs	Exploring coping competencies	1, 3	MS	10	109
Mindful Breathing	Whole Circle	A calming strategy to reduce anxiety and stress	3	YMS	3	27
Mirrored Emotions	Pairs	Showing how contagious emotions are	2	YMS	6	53
Monologues and Dialogues	Pairs	Experiencing and practising conversation	5	MS	5	44
Moods and Music	Small Groups	How things around us influence feelings	2	YMS	6	60
Mrs Mumbleby	Whole Circle	A game in the round to stimulate laughter	4, 8	YMS	7	69
My Favourite Things	Pairs	Topics for shared conversations	5	YMS	5	42
Names on a Train	Whole Circle	An active game to include everyone	4, 7	YM	3	24
Newspaper Game	Small Groups	Creating order from chaos – together	4, 5, 7	MS	9	89

(Continued)

(Continued)

Name	Who for?	Description	SEL Dimension(s)	YMS	Ch.	Page
Noises Off	Small Groups	Making a tape of sounds for others to guess	5, 9	YMS	5	46
Now and Then	Whole Circle	Are historical concepts still relevant?	2	S	6	56
One Word Categories	Whole Circle	Attention and thinking, learning to lose	5, 1	YMS	5	47
Optimistic Conversations	Pairs	Focusing on things to cherish and hope for	5,8	YMS	7	64
Our Class	Small Groups	A flag or shield collage to represent the class	4, 5	YM	8	78
Over the Top and Back Again	Whole Circle	Showing different strengths of various emotions		MS	6	55
P-Charts	Small Groups	Dimensions of bullying and intervention	10, 11	MS	10	100
Paddlepop Positives	Whole Circle	Looking out for the positives in others	4, 8	YM	4	34
Pass It On Gotcha Cards	Whole Circle	Acknowledgement for friendly behaviours	5	YM	9	94
Passing Clouds	Whole Circle	Practising detachment and mindfulness	3	YMS	5	41
People Music	Whole Circle	Energizer and belonging	4	YMS	5	45
Personal Bests	Pairs	How to always be a winner	8	YMS	4	33
Perspective Glasses	Whole Circle	Leadership in identifying strengths in others	4, 7	YM	4	39
Perspectives	Small Groups	Understanding different ways of seeing things	1, 3, 8	MS	7	64
Pick a Picture	Whole Circle	A game to reflect on learning	1	MS	3	30
Picture Me	Whole Circle	Getting to know each other	5	MS	8	72
Picture My Values	Whole Circle	Using photos to identify what is important in life	1, 12	MS	4	37
Post-It Pride	Pairs	Identifying strengths in others, listening skills	4, 5, 6	S	4	33
Punch lines	Small Groups	Sharing a joke – healthy laughter	4, 8	YM	7	69

Name	Who for?	Description	SEL Dimension(s)	YMS	Ch.	Page
Puppets	Small Groups	Using puppets to stimulate discussion on ethos	9, 10, 11	Y	10	96
Purple World	Whole Circle	The need for diversity – addressing racism	4, 11	Y	8	74
Random Acts of Kindness	Whole Circle	Acknowledging and talking about kindness	2, 5	MS	9	92
Ready, Steady, Stop	Small Groups	Understanding and dealing with anger	2,3	YMS	10	107
Recipe for a Safe and Happy Class	Small Groups	Everyone is responsible for class atmosphere	6, 7, 11	YM	10	99
Rescue!	Whole Circle	Energizer for group cooperation and support	5, 11	M	8	75
Rights and Responsibilities	Small Groups	Each right comes with a responsibility to others	1, 4, 11	MS	9	91
Sadness and Depression	Whole Circle	Showing the difference between the two	2	MS	10	109
Scavenger Hunt	Small Groups	Everyone playing a part – taking responsibility	4, 5	MS	9	89
Sea, Shore and Sharks	Whole Circle	Energizer, promoting team spirit	8	YM	3	27
Secret Friend	Whole Circle	Friendship in action for individuals	4, 5	YMS	9	87
Seeing Is Hearing	Whole Circle	Empathy with hearing impairment	4, 6	MS	8	79
Shared Blame	Pairs	Taking appropriate responsibility	3, 8, 9	MS	7	64
Silence or Support	Small Groups	Bystander intervention in bullying	1, 6, 11	MS	10	101
Silent Construction	Small Groups	Decision-making and cooperation	5, 7	YMS	9	88
Single Word Stories	Whole Circle	Working together to construct a story	5	MS	5	47
Sleeping Lions	Whole Circle	Calming activity for young children	2	Y	3	29
Snowball Fight	Whole Circle	Qualities of a good friend, energizer	5, 8	MS	9	87
Social Bingo	Whole Circle	Finding out what you share and what is different	4, 5	MS	5	45

(Continued)

(Continued)

Name	Who for?	Description	SEL Dimension(s)	YMS	Ch.	Page
Soft Balls	Whole Circle	Connecting with names, focusing attention	5	YMS	3	23
Something About You	Whole Circle	Exploring similarities and differences	4	YMS	8	74
Sounds	Whole Circle	Listening and mindfulness, being in the moment	2, 8	YMS	3	28
Special People	Pairs	Emotional impact of communication	2	YMS	6	52
Speed Dating	Whole Circle	Practising conversation	5	MS	9	85
Spoon Race	Whole Circle	Cooperation in teams, laughter	4, 5, 8	YMS	9	87
Stand Up, Turn Round, Sit Down Stories	Whole Circle	Energizer, promotes listening and attention skills	5, 8	YMS	3	27
Star of the Day	Whole Circle	Focusing on strengths one child at a time	4, 8	YM	4	34
Sticky Labels Teamwork	Small Groups	Understanding how we operate in a group	4, 5	MS	5	48
Stories	Pairs or Small Groups	Using stories to address sensitive issues safely	9, 10, 11	YMS	10	96
Strength Cards	Whole Circle	Multiple activities	1, 8	YMS	4	33
Strength Gotcha	Whole Circle	Embedding a strengths approach	4, 5	YM	4	39
Strength Statues	Small Groups	Talking about and representing strengths	1, 5, 8	YMS	4	34
Strengths Stories	Small Groups	What strengths look like in practice, role-play	5, 8	MS	4	34
Stretching	Whole Circle	Relaxation exercise	3	YMS	3	28
Success Stories	Small Groups	Reflections on what is really important in life	1, 12	S	7	68
Superpowers	Small Groups	Strengths you need for different situations	5, 6	MS	4	35
Swapping Sides	Pairs	Role-playing opposing positions	9, 10	MS	10	105
Taking Care of Teddy	Small Groups	Discussing ethos and action with young children	6, 11	Y	10	100

Name	Who for?	Description	SEL Dimension(s)	YMS	Ch.	Page
Tense and Release	Whole Circle	Relaxation exercise	3	YMS	3	28
Thanks in a Hat	Small Groups	Acknowledging and thanking those who help	5, 8	YMS	7	68
The Drawing Challenge	Small Groups	Empathy with physical difficulties	4, 6	YMS	8	79
The Drawing Game	Whole Circle	Team work promoting divergent thinking	5, 7, 8	YMS	5	47
The 100 Person Village	Whole Circle	What do we have compared to others?	4, 11, 12	S	8	73
The Jelly Wobble	Whole Circle	Empathy with visual impairment, laughter	6, 8	YM	8	78
The Last Straw	Small Groups	Dealing with stress	2, 3	MS	10	108
The Laughter Chain	Whole Circle	Showing how contagious laughter can be	4, 8	YM	7	69
The Mask	Small Groups	Different ways we present to the world	2, 3, 6	MS	6	59
The Sixth Sense	Whole Circle	Understanding people with social impairment	2, 6	M	8	80
The Smile	Whole Circle	To show that smiles are stronger than frowns	2, 3	Y	6	54
The War for Wellbeing	Pairs or Small Groups	Personalizing positive and negative self-talk	1, 3, 8	YMS	7	65
The Warm Wind Blows	Whole Circle	Energizer and mix up. Everyone loves this game!	4, 5, 7	YMS	3	26
Worm Game	Whole Circle	For young pupils to promote belonging in a class	4, 8	Y	8	82
Think Again – Uses For …	Small Groups	Promoting divergent thinking in a group	5, 8	MS	9	91
This Class Cares	Small Groups	Maximizing inclusion and taking responsibility	4, 8	YMS	8	78
This Class Says Thank You	Small Groups	Promoting thankfulness across the school	4, 8	YMS	7	68
This Is Me – and Me – and Me	Pairs	Awareness of different roles	1	MS	4	37
Time Capsule	Whole Circle	Reflecting on your world and what is meaningful	1, 11, 12	MS	4	38
True or False	Small Groups	Identifying the complexity of many situations	6, 7	MS	9	91

(Continued)

(Continued)

Name	Who for?	Description	SEL Dimension(s)	YMS	Ch.	Page
Valuing You	Whole Circle	Identifying what you value in others	4, 5	MS	4	38
Visiting Strange Lands	Whole Circle	To appreciate difficulties newcomers may have	4, 5, 6	MS	8	81
Warmer … Louder	Whole Circle	Whole Circle cooperation	4, 5	YM	9	86
What Do We Know?	Small Groups	Learning not to pre-judge on limited information	3, 6	MS	8	75
What If This Happened to You?	Whole Circle	Role-play an incident of cyber-bullying	6, 9, 10	MS	10	101
What Would You Notice?	Small Groups	A narrative 'externalizing' approach to feelings	2, 3	MS	6	58
Where Is the Feeling Now?	Small Groups	Looking at emotions on a continuum	2, 3	MS	6	58
Who Says What?	Pairs	Determining useful and less useful thinking	1, 8	YMS	7	68
Who's in Charge?	Whole Circle	Body awareness	2, 3	YM	3	28
Why My Name?	Pairs or Whole Circle	Stories about our names	4, 5	YMS	3	24
Worry Warts	Pairs	What grows or diminishes anxiety	2, 3	YMS	10	108

Appendix 3
Useful Resources

Organizations Promoting Wellbeing for Young People

The following organizations in North America, the UK and Australia provide information on one or more of the following: wellbeing, social and emotional learning, whole school/whole child approaches to education, anti-bullying, restorative practices.

Edutopia: Empowering and connecting teachers, administrators and parents with innovative solutions and resources to better education. Lots of great ideas and resources including video clips about what works in education: www.edutopia.org

The New Economics Foundation: An independent think-and-do tank that inspires and demonstrates real economic wellbeing, including wellbeing indicators and measurement: www.neweconomics.org/publications/entry/five-ways-to-well-being-the-evidence

1. **Connect** – With the people around you. With family, friends, colleagues and neighbours.
2. **Be Active** – Go for a walk or run. Step outside. Cycle. Play a game. Garden. Dance.
3. **Take Notice** – Be curious. Appreciate what matters to you.
4. **Keep Learning** – This will help make you more confident as well as being fun.
5. **Give** – Do something nice for a friend or a stranger. Thank someone. Smile.

Young Minds: The UK's leading charity committed to improving the emotional wellbeing and mental health of children and young people: www.youngminds.org.uk

The Children's Society: www.childrenssociety.org.uk - Their page on promoting positive wellbeing for children can be found here: bit.ly/117X0P8

MindMatters: Mental health promotion in Australian secondary schools: www.mindmatters.edu.au. Includes a page on Staff Matters and teacher wellbeing.

KidsMatter: Mental health and wellbeing framework for primary schools across Australia: www.kidsmatter.edu.au

Wellbeing Australia: Wellbeing Australia is committed to developing the resilience, relationships and responsibility that lead to individual and community wellbeing, especially in education: www.wellbeingaustralia.com.au/wba – now in partnership with ARACY to form SWAN (see below).

The Collaborative for Academic, Social and Emotional Learning: Much of the evidence on SEL is published by CASEL researchers – well worth a look if you need to convince anyone of the need: casel.org

The Australian Alliance for Children and Young People – ARACY promotes several initiatives to improve the wellbeing of young Australians, specifically the NEST (a national plan for child and youth wellbeing) and SWAN (Student Wellbeing Action Network): www.aracy.org.au

NICE: National Institute for Health and Clinical Excellence – pathways to wellbeing: bit.ly/12mNG1l

Anti-Bullying Alliance: Creating safe environments in which children can live, grow, play and learn. In partnership with the National Children's Bureau in the UK: www.anti-bullyingalliance.org.uk

Safe Schools hub – working together to build safe and supportive schools: www.safeschoolshub.edu.au

National Centre Against Bullying creating caring communities for children: www.ncab.org.au

Greater Good: The science of a meaningful life: organization based at Berkeley University in the USA – great information and video clips: greatergood.berkeley.edu/gg-live

Roots of Empathy: Changing the world, child by child. This organization is based in Canada: www.rootsofempathy.org.uk

School Climate: Educating minds and hearts because the three Rs are not enough: www.schoolclimate.org

Safer Saner Schools: Restorative practices: www.safersanerschools.org (USA)

Transforming Conflict: National Centre for Restorative Approaches in Youth Settings (UK): www.transformingconflict.org

British Council: Best Practice Guidelines for Diversity and Inclusion in Education: www.britishcouncil.org/malta-indie-best-practice-guidelines.pdf

Circle Solutions website: www.circlesolutionsnetwork.com/csn – for information about training and new resources. You can also leave comments and share ideas here.

Material Resources for Use in Circles

St Luke's Innovative Resources have a large selection of beautifully produced materials that have a wide range of uses in Circles. These include strength cards for different ages, strengths in circles (the CS principles), community strengths, emotions, relational values, futures and many more. All come with a leaflet giving ideas on possible uses but creative teachers will be able to develop even more. Based in Australia, they deliver globally: www.innovativeresources.org

SEAL: Social and Emotional Aspects of Learning UK – archived materials can be found here: bit.ly/ZzLban

Inyahead Press have cards, stickers, posters and other materials that support Circle activities as well as many related books: www.inyahead.com.au

Kimochi dolls – soft toys that help young children learn about their feelings and how to manage them: www.kimochis.co.uk or www.kimochis.com.au

The Quirky Kid Clinic produces resources primarily for use by therapists and counsellors but several work well for Circle activities – great illustrations: therapeuticresources.com.au/quirky-kid-pack

Game Time: Games to Promote Social and Emotional Resilience for Children Aged 4 to 14 by Robyn Hromek (London: Lucky Duck, Sage). This includes a CD with board games that you can print out. Great for small group work.

Yarnabout: 75 powerful photographic images for story-telling, building conversations and reflection, especially with Aboriginal students. Developed by the Nungeena Aboriginal Corporation.

Internet Resources for Circle Games

(Choose carefully to ensure activities are congruent with CS principles!)

bit.ly/19x9cAG – cooperative games PDF from the Primary Professional Development Service in Dublin.

bit.ly/15rGzSg – Peace Games network – new games go up on this site every month.

www.ultimatecampresource.com/site/camp-activities/circle-games.page-4.html

www.gameskidsplay.net/games/circle_games/

www.primaryresources.co.uk/pshe/pdfs/dramawarmups.pdf

www.kidscount1234.com/circlegames.html

talisker.hubpages.com/hub/Circle-time-games-and-activities-A-must-for-any-teacher (these have learning objectives attached).

www.activityvillage.co.uk/ice-breaker_games.htm (for children who don't know each other).

www.schoolslinkingnetwork.org.uk/wp-content/uploads/2011/07/Circle-Games-and-Warm-ups.pdf

www.youthwork-practice.com/games/circle-games.html

iteslj.org/games (has activities for students with English as a second language).

www.wilderdom.com

Anti-Defamation League. This US website has ideas for promoting respect for diversity, including multiculturalism and additional needs inclusion: www.adl.org/education/curriculum_connections

Circle Books

These are just the ones I know about – there many more – just Google!

For All Ages

Armstrong, M. and Vinegrad, D. (2013) *Working in Circles in Primary and Secondary Classrooms.* Melbourne, Australia: Inyahead Press

Bellhouse, B. (2008) *The Circle Time Games and Activities Resources Kit.* Melbourne: Inyahead Press. This pack contains cards for use in games.

Bellhouse, B. (2011) *Developing Resilience with Circle Time.* Melbourne: Inyahead Press

Bliss, T. and Tetley, J. (2004) *Circle Time: A Resource Book for Primary and Secondary Schools.* London: Lucky Duck, Sage.

Rogers, V. (2011) *Games and Activities for Exploring Feelings with Children.* London: Jessica Kingsley – for 7–13-year-olds.

White, M. (2008) *Magic Circles: Building Self-Esteem through Circle Time*, Second Edition. London: Lucky Duck, Sage.

Games, Games, Games: A Co-operative Games Book – available from the Woodcraft website: woodcraft.org.uk/images/games-games-games-book

The Early Years

Collins, M. (2011) *Circle Time for the Very Young*, Third Edition. London: Lucky Duck, Sage.

Collins, M. (2003) *Enhancing Circle Time for the Very Young.* London: Lucky Duck, Sage.

Mosley, J. (2006) *Circle Time for Young Children.* London: Routledge.

Weatherhead, Y. (2008) *Creative Circle Time Lessons for the Early Years.* London: Lucky Duck, Sage.

Primary Schools

Curry, M. and Bromfield, C. (2004) *Personal and Social Education for Primary Schools through Circle Time.* Tamworth, Staffs: NASEN.

Davies, G. (1999) *Six Years of Circle Time.* London: Lucky Duck, Sage.

Davies, G. (2004) *Six More Years of Circle Time.* London: Lucky Duck, Sage.

Hansberry, B. and Langley, J. (2013) *The Grab and Go Circle Time Kit for Teaching Restorative Behaviour.* Melbourne: Inyahead.

Mosley, J. (1996) *Quality Circle Time in the Primary Classroom.* Hyde: LDA Learning

Secondary Schools

Mosley, J. and Tew, M. (2013) *Quality Circle Time in the Secondary School.* London: David Fulton Publishers, Taylor and Francis.

Smith, C. (2003) *Circle Time for Secondary Students* (series of three). London: Lucky Duck, Sage.

Tew, M., Read, M. and Potter, H. (2007) *Circles PSHE and Citizenship.* London: Lucky Duck, Sage.

Books with Ideas Adaptable for Circles

Bowkett, S. (1999) *Self-Intelligence: A Handbook for Developing Confidence, Self-Esteem and Interpersonal Skills.* Stafford: Network Educational Press. A wealth of activities for working with individual students that could easily be done in pairs.

Brunskill, K. (2006) *Learning to be Honest, Kind and Friendly for 5–7-year-olds*. London: Lucky Duck, Sage

Brunskill, K. (2006) *Developing Consideration, Respect and Tolerance for 7–9-year-olds*. London: Lucky Duck, Sage.

Brunskill, K. (2006) *Enhancing Courage, Respect and Assertiveness for 9–12-year-olds*. London: Lucky Duck, Sage.

Corrie, C. (2009) *Becoming Emotionally Intelligent*. Varsity Lakes, Qld: Network Educational Press.

Fuller, A., Bellhouse, B. and Johnston, G. (2001) *The Heart Masters: A Program for the Promotion of Emotional Intelligence and Resilience*. Melbourne: Inyahead Press. Three books for lower primary, middle and upper primary and junior secondary.

Greef, A. (2005) *Resilience, Vol. 1: Personal Skills for Effective Learning*. Carmarthen: Crown House Publishing.

Lewkowicz, A. (2008) *Teaching Emotional Intelligence*. Melbourne: Hawker Brownlow.

McGrath, H. and Noble, T. (2011) *Bounce Back: A Classroom Resiliency Program*. Melbourne: Pearson Education. Three books for lower primary, middle and upper primary and junior secondary.

Moore, C. and Rae, T. (2000) *Positive People: A Self-Esteem Building Course for Young Children*. London: Lucky Duck, Sage.

Rae, T. (2008) *Good Choices Teaching Young People Aged 8–11 to Make Positive Decisions about Their Own Lives*. London: Lucky Duck, Sage.

Rae, T., Nakara, N. and Velinor, P. (2011) *Emotional Resilience and Problem-Solving: Promote the Mental Health and Wellbeing for Young Adults*. London: Optimus Education

Warden, D. and Christie, D (2001) *Teaching Social Behaviour: Classroom Activities to Teach Social Awareness*. London: David Fulton Publishers, Taylor and Francis. Cartoon scenarios for discussion. For all ages.

Books for Discussing Issues

There are thousands of stories to promote thinking and talking about issues – here are just a few. Explore others on the websites at the end of this list.

Bornman, J., Collins, M. and Maines, B. (2004) *Just the Same on the Inside. Understanding Diversity and Supporting Inclusion in Circle Time*. London: Lucky Duck, Sage. For primary students.

Collins, M. (2005) *It's OK to Be Sad*. London: Lucky Duck, Sage. Book for 4–9-year-olds containing 20 stories about different and difficult life events.

Ingouville, F. (2005) *On the Same Side: 133 Stories to Help Resolve Conflict*. London: Lucky Duck, Sage. For all ages.

Ironside, V. (2011) *The Huge Bag of Worries*. London: Hodder Children's Books. For primary students.

Leicester, M. (2005) *Stories for Circle Time and Assembly: Developing Literacy Skills and Classroom Values*. London: Routledge Falmer. For younger students.

Mathr, M. and Yeowart, E. (2004) *The Crescent: Stories to Introduce the Concept of Moral Values for Children aged 5–7*. London: Lucky Duck, Sage.

McCloud, C., Wells, K. and Weber, P. (2012) *Will You Fill My Bucket? Daily Acts of Love Around the World*. Northville, MI: Nelson Publishing and Marketing. For primary aged children.

McCloud, C., Martin, K. and Messing, D. (2009) *Fill a Bucket. A Guide to Daily Happiness for Young Children*. Northville, MI: Nelson Publishing and Marketing.

Munroe, E. A. (2010) *The Anxiety Workbook for Girls*. Minneapolis, MN: Fairview Press. Upper primary and secondary.

Nunn, T. (2008) *The Who's Who of the Brain: A Guide to its Inhabitants*. London: Jessica Kingsley. Some valuable and accessible neuropsychology for more senior students.

Weatherhead, Y. (2004) *Enriching Circle Time: Dream Journeys and Positive Thoughts*. London: Lucky Duck, Sage. Primary and lower secondary.

Peoplemaking has an impressive list of books on a wide variety of social and emotional issues for students of all ages, teachers and parents: peoplemaking.com.au

Pinterest is an online pinboard – a sharing site with one section devoted to story books for learning about life and its challenges including such issues as fathers in jail, parental separation and losing a pet: pinterest.com/pamdyson/social-emotional-books/

References

Bandura, Albert (1986) *Social Foundations of Thought and Action*. Englewood Cliffs, NJ: Prentice-Hall.

Benard, Bonnie (2004) *Resiliency: What We Have Learned*. San Francisco: WestEd.

Bronfenbrenner, Urie (1979) *The Ecology of Human Development: Experiences by Nature and Design*. Cambridge, MA: Harvard University Press.

Cohen, Jonathan (2006) 'Social, emotional, ethical, and academic education: creating a climate for learning, participation in democracy, and wellbeing', *Harvard Educational Review*, 76(2): 201–37.

Craig, C. (2007) *The Potential Dangers of a Systematic, Explicit Approach to Teaching Social and Emotional Skills*. Centre for Confidence and Wellbeing. (www.centreforconfidence.co.uk/docs/SEALsummary.pdf)

Ecclestone, Kathryn and Hayes, Dennis (2008) *The Dangerous Rise of Therapeutic Education*. London: Routledge.

Elias, Maurice J. (2010) 'Sustainability of social-emotional learning and related programs: lessons from a field study', *International Journal of Emotional Education*, 2(1): 17–33.

Elias, Maurice J., Zins, Joseph E., Graczyk, Patricia A. and Weissberg, Roger P. (2003) 'Implementation, sustainability, and scaling up of social-emotional and academic innovations in public schools', *School Psychology Review*, 32(3): 303–19.

Fredrickson, Barbara (2011) *Positivity: Ground-Breaking Research to Release Your Inner Optimist and Thrive*. Oxford: OneWorld Publications.

Gable, Shelly L., Reis, Harry T., Impett, Emily A. and Asher, Evan R. (2004) 'What do you do when things go right? The intrapersonal and interpersonal benefits of sharing positive events', *Journal of Personality and Social Psychology*, 87: 228–45.

Gilligan, Carol (1982) *In a Different Voice: Psychological Theory and Women's Development*. Cambridge, MA: Harvard University Press.

Glasser, William (1997) '"Choice Theory" and student success', *Education Digest*, 63(3): 16–21.

Hansberry, Bill and Langley, Jane (2012) *The Grab and Go Circle Time Kit for Teaching Restorative Behaviour*. Melbourne: Inyahead Press.

Horsch, Patricia, Chen, Jie-Qi and Wagner, Suzanna L. (2002) 'The responsive classroom approach: a caring, respectful school environment as a context for development', *Education and Urban Society*, 34(3): 365–83.

Ishikawa, Kaoru (1980 [original Japanese edition 1970]) *QC Circle Koryo: General Principles of the QC Circle*. Tokyo: QC Circle Headquarters, Union of Japanese Scientists and Engineers.

Keyes, Corey L.M. and Haidt, Jonathan (2003) *Flourishing: Positive Psychology and the Life Well-Lived*. Washington, DC: American Psychological Association.

Kohlberg, Lawrence and Turiel, Elliot (1971) 'Moral development and moral education', in Lawrence Kohlberg, *Collected Papers on Moral Development and Moral Education* (1973), pp. 410–65.

MacLure, Maggie, Jones, Liz, Holmes, Rachel and MacRae, Christina (2012) 'Becoming a problem: behaviour and reputation in the early years classroom', *British Educational Research Journal*, 38: 447–71. (onlinelibrary.wiley.com/doi/10.1080/01411926.2011.552709/abstract)

McCarthy, Florence E. (2009) *Circle Time Solutions: Creating Caring School Communities: An Analysis of a Learning through Community Service Initiative Supporting Circle Time in Eight Primary Schools in Greater Western Sydney*. Sydney: NSW Department of Education and Training.

Mosco, Jane and O'Brien, Kimberley (2012) 'Positive parent–child relationships', in Sue Roffey (ed.), *Positive Relationships: Evidence Based Practice Across the World*. Dordrecht: Springer Verlag.

Murray, Judith (2004) 'Making sense of resilience: a useful step on the road to creating and maintaining resilient students and school communities', *Australian Journal of Guidance and Counselling*, 14(1): 1–15.

Noble, Toni, McGrath, Helen, Roffey, Sue and Rowling, Louise (2008) *A Scoping Study on Student Wellbeing.* Canberra, ACT: Department of Education, Employment and Workplace Relations.

Noddings, Nel (2002) *Educating Moral People: A Caring Alternative to Character Education.* New York: Teachers College Press.

Potter, Jonathan (1996) *Representing Reality: Discourse, Rhetoric and Social Construction.* London: Sage.

Rigby, Ken and Bagshaw, Dale (2006) 'Using educational drama and bystander training to counteract bullying', in Helen McGrath and Toni Noble (eds), *Bullying Solutions: Evidence-Based Approaches to Bullying in Australian Schools.* Melbourne: Pearson Education. pp. 133–46.

Roffey, Sue (2004) 'The home–school interface for behaviour: a conceptual framework for co-constructing reality', *Educational and Child Psychology*, 21(4): 95–108.

Roffey, Sue (2010) 'Content and context for learning relationships: a cohesive framework for individual and whole school development', *Educational and Child Psychology*, 27(1): 156–67.

Roffey, Sue (2011) *Changing Behaviour in Schools: Promoting Relationships and Wellbeing.* London: Sage.

Roffey, Sue (2012a) 'Student wellbeing: teacher wellbeing: two sides of the same coin', *Educational and Child Psychology*, 29(4): 8–17.

Roffey, Sue (ed.) (2012b) *Positive Relationships: Evidence-Based Practice Across the World.* Dordrecht: Springer Verlag.

Roffey, Sue and Hromek, Robyn (2009) 'Games as a pedagogy for social and emotional learning. "It's fun and we learn things"', *Simulation and Gaming*, 40(5): 626–44.

Roffey, Sue and McCarthy, Florence E. (2013) 'Circle Solutions: a philosophy and pedagogy for learning positive relationships. What promotes and inhibits sustainable outcomes?', *International Journal of Emotional Education*, 5(1): 36–55.

Seligman, Martin E.P. (2011) *Flourish: A New Understanding of Happiness and Well-Being – and How To Achieve Them.* New York: Free Press.

Skiba, Russell J., Reynolds, Cecil R., Graham, Sandra, Sheras, Peter, Close Conely, Jane and Garcia-Vasquez, Enedina (2006) *Are Zero Tolerance Policies Effective in the Schools? An Evidentiary Review and Recommendations.* Zero Tolerance Task Force Report for the American Psychological Association.

Vygotsky, Lev S. (1978) *Mind in Society: Development of Higher Psychological Processes.* Cambridge, MA: Harvard University Press.

Wilkinson, Richard and Pickett, Kate (2010) *The Spirit Level: Why Equality Is Better for Everyone.* London: Penguin.

Zins, Joseph E., Weissberg, Roger P., Wang, Margaret C. and Walber, Herbert J. (2004) *Building Academic Success on Social and Emotional Learning: What Does the Research Say?* New York: Teachers College Press.

Index